The DON'T Before I Do

EMILY McKNIGHT

The Don't Before I Do

The opinions and conclusions expressed in this book are those of the author. As for personal examples and scenarios from the author's life, the names and some circumstances were altered for purposes of privacy.

Editors: Brian Sandy and Stefanie Manns
Cover Designer: Kanika Harris

To my beautiful daughters…

May you never question a man's love for you and may whatever mistakes you make in relationships be your own and not replicas of mine. My testimony is not in vain, and the two of you are perfect examples of God's grace. Love is…US.

For my Forever Love

No one will ever know the depth of our love. We trusted God and are still reaping the rewards. Just think, where this story ends, is just the beginning for us. You and me…invincible.

TABLE *of* CONTENTS

Prelude

HELLO, MY NAME IS EMILY

...and I'm a...Hopeless Romantic. Yeah, that's probably the best way to describe myself. I love LOVE. Always have and always will. The feeling that surfaced around age thirteen lasted for almost two decades, until I was blessed with the man I was destined to marry and love for the rest of my life, God willing. Well, what did I do for the twenty years prior? I'll tell you—I fell in love over and over and over again with the "perfect guy," only to find out he was the "not-so-perfect guy," and sometimes even the "worst guy in the world." One thing is for sure: I never ever gave up on love. I was your typical serial dater, never having gone longer than a year or so without being in a serious relationship.

I've read almost every self-help book on relationships, watched hundreds of romantic dramas and movies, and I've even taken a series of seminars and live classes about dating. Not to mention my music therapy, getting lost in every love song imaginable, from any and every genre or era. Yet it still took me twenty years to figure things out. But once I did, girl, let me tell you, it was like I had a superpower, like I was invincible. I started having the best dating experiences of my life. It may have been the extensive research, or it may have been the strong yearning for love, but I was super single and loving the dating scene- the same scene I couldn't stand just months prior.

At the end of the day, I don't think I spent twenty years in and out of relationships in vain. I think the day that I married the man of my dreams, July 27, 2014, was the exact date I was supposed to. I feel that I had to endure every experience, every breakup, every heartache, every emotional roller coaster, so that one day I would come in contact with YOU, my sister, to coach you as your virtual girlfriend and give you the tools to make your dating experiences ten times better, and to drastically reduce your dating time and get you to that altar. There is no reason for you to repeat the same mistakes I made.

Throughout this book, I outline every significant relationship I had, and the lessons I learned from those relationships. My hopes are for you to either identify yourself in my relationships and experiences and take the lessons learned, or to educate you on these scenarios so if they were to come your way, you would know exactly how to handle yourself. Or perhaps you have surpassed this level and are in a good place with respect to dating, and you just need a few tips to either meet men, improve your interaction with them, or maximize your experience with the man you are currently dating. If that's you, I can shed some light on your situation, too.

I have no doubt that I was placed on this earth to hold your hand through this process, to eliminate some of the baggage and hurt that can go from one relationship to the other if not handled correctly, and cheer you on until you meet the love of your life.

Now, as for marriage and what to do when you become a wife, that's a different story. I'm trying to figure out that "wife life" right now myself. But I will tell you this—the day your arguments shift from late nights out, strip clubs, and inappropriate DMs to "How come you didn't make my smoothie with love like you did yours?" is the exact day you will thank me.

Seriously, what I will share with you will be the truth, my story and all of its craziness, hoping you will be blessed and encouraged by it. Now I must warn you, I wish it was as simple as saying, "Girlfriend, do this and do that…" and voila! Your husband shows up. No, actually, it was quite the opposite for me. What if I told you that the turning point in my dating experiences were what I *stopped* doing? The things I *didn't* do? It was essentially the DON'T before I DO that led me to that altar. Wait, don't be alarmed or worried. Don't close the book up just yet. I walk you through it all, each relationship, each epiphany, each turn of obedience and the results there after.

As you read these words, your husband is being prepared by the Almighty. Until He delivers that man to you, the focus will be on you, my dear. The moment you even remotely see yourself in my story, perk up, listen, and take notes. I'll give you the play by play on how things changed for the better. I'll teach you everything I know now and wish I'd known then about how to find a loving, lasting relationship. And I'll definitely share what you need to do to get there. Just think, if a relationship were a song, I'm here to give you the lyrics. Imagine how much better the melody would sound, if only you knew the words. Along the way, I promise you'll laugh out loud and may even shed a tear or two. These pages, sweetheart, is as real as it gets.

But know this—if it worked for me, it can work for you. To all of my hopeless fellow romantics out there, I want you to know that there is hope. Now let's get you to that altar, shall we?

Chapter 1
IF IT ISN'T LOVE

Love. What does it look like? What does it feel like? Taste, sound, even smell like? I was so curious about this thing called love. Not the love you receive from your mom and dad, or your siblings, but the love between a man and a woman. The love you see and hear portrayed on TV and in music. I wanted to be a part of it. I wanted to be loved, and to give love.

I spent most of my pre-teen years fantasizing about the notion of love, from watching boys playing basketball and daydreaming that they were my guy, to having endless conversations with my childhood friends about what my boyfriend would look like, what my husband would do for a living, and what we would name our five children. By the eighth grade, it wasn't uncommon to hear about classmates "talking" to one another, making out, and experimenting with sex, and some of them were fully sexually active. I used to think, *Wow! They are so in love.* Very soon, I started equating sex and sexuality with love.

Fast-forward a few years, and I am on my way from Los Angeles, California to Forrest City, Arkansas. You heard me? From sunny Cali, city of the stars, to a town that no one has heard of deep in the South, in the state of Arkansas of all states. My mother, newly divorced, had returned to her deceased mother's hometown to rebuild her mother's home and start a new life with her new boyfriend. Being the youngest daughter of three girls, with both sisters now adults and out of the house, I had the good fortune of being able to delay going with my mother by staying with my eldest sister, Lynette, for a year or two before having to move when she got married, starting her own life anew. Perhaps it was best that my mom raised her own kid. There were some feelings of rejection there, I must admit. But, in hindsight, it made sense. So off I went, to join my mom on her escapade.

It wasn't like I hadn't lived in Arkansas before. When my grandmother was alive, I had spent many summers there and, on a couple of occasions, small stints during the school year. At that time, I was between the ages of five and ten. This time, the move was different. No one has a life at that age. I was now fourteen, entering my second year of high school, and moving to Arkansas. Disaster!

I should probably mention at this point that my mother and I had a very fragile relationship, having spent a few years apart. You see, my mother was bipolar, manic depressive, with alternating highs and lows, episodes of mania and severe depression.

Once I arrived in Arkansas, it dawned on me that I was entering a land that no one had dwelled in before—one-on-one time with my mom. Just me and her. No sisters, no Dad, no Granny to come to my rescue in the time of need.

When I arrived, my mother was in good spirits during a "normal" period, so I decided to make the best of it. The summer before school started, she and I had a great ol' time fixing up my new room, and staying up late playing cards and watching movies. She even taught me how to drive on the dirt roads. We really connected for a minute; I felt loved by my mother again. I had missed that.

Then her boyfriend returned to Arkansas from a trip out of town. He was always very strange to me. He changed the entire dynamic of our house every time he was around. When things were cheerful and happy, he found a way to bring the atmosphere down, talking about my not doing the dishes right, or how many hours I spent on the phone. He found any and everything to complain to my mother about me. I felt that oh-so-familiar feeling again. As if he didn't want me there, like I was in the way. Needless to say, the blue skies of Arkansas were cloudy again.

On the first day of school, I really didn't know what to expect. I wondered if any of the kids I went to elementary school with would remember me. I doubted it. I wondered if my outfit and hair were okay. I was one hundred percent self-conscious.

The moment I stepped foot in the door, I experienced an immediate culture shock. I looked at the girls in the hallway. They were dressed totally different than I was, different hairstyles, different shoes. I stuck out like a sore thumb. As I walked through the halls, listening to the conversations, everyone sounded funny. Even when I asked for directions to my homeroom, I couldn't understand them, nor could they understand me—and I talked proper.

I was an alien on another planet. For about ten minutes.

Then there was an immediate paradigm shift. Once I got past comparing myself to every female I came across, I started hearing whispers as I walked past, and saw the guys elbowing their friends to get their attention.

Considering Forrest City is a small town, of course everyone knew each other or grew up together. So once my unfamiliar face came through that door, it was all eyes on me. Yes, me. The chubby girl with the pretty face that didn't get much play in Los Angeles walked through those school doors and felt like she was Aaliyah or somebody, turning guys' heads as she walked by. The bold ones were outright walking up to me, asking my name, where I was from, complimenting me, asking for my number. I turn down one, and another one would quickly follow. I had never experienced that before, but it didn't take too long to get used to that kind of attention. As time went on, I was getting the hang of things. Met a few new friends, ran into a few old ones.

Things were simple in Forrest City. There, they did the same thing week in and week out: Friday night—football or basketball game; Saturday night—anybody's guess; Sunday night—skating rink. I recall one Friday evening sitting with my friends at the football game and seeing this guy walk through the crowd. He seemed pretty popular, since quite a few people spoke to him as he walked by. I thought he was very cute—light-skinned, light eyes, curly hair, muscular, kind of short, which was okay, since I was short, too.

I knew I hadn't seen him before at school. So, of course, I asked my friend, "Who's that?"

"Oh, that's Mason," she said. "He graduated last year. Pretty good basketball player."

I followed up with, "He is *cuuuuttttteeee*."

Next thing I know, the guy was sitting next to me. That's how fast that happened. That's how they did things in the South—no hinting, no beating around the bush, no walking past the guy fifty times until he noticed you. It's more like, "Oh, you like him? Cool, let me go tell him."

Well, we talked for a few minutes, and he told me he was eighteen. Now I was fourteen and had never really talked to a guy that much older than me before. Actually, I'd never had a serious boyfriend up until this point, so I was pretty inexperienced. What I did know was, I was infatuated with love, and sexuality meant love, and I figured that's what I needed to relay to finally get that love.

So when he asked if our age would be a problem, I responded like Aaliyah, "No. Age ain't nothin' but a number."

Our next encounter was that Sunday, at the skating rink. I made sure I looked very cute, and mature, with my perfume on and pink Jordana lipstick. What I do remember about our second interaction was that the conversation focused on the physical very quickly.

He point-blank asked me, "Are you a virgin?"

Quickly, I responded, "Hell no!", which of course was a lie.

With those pretty hazel eyes, he looked at me. "All right then. Bet."

The following Tuesday evening, we were over our church family's house for dinner. Somehow, we talked our parents into going on to Bible study while the kids stayed behind. I remember asking my friend, who was slightly older, closer to Mason's age, if she knew him, and of course she did. I asked if it was okay if he came by, and she agreed.

Didn't take long for him to drive over. And all that Aaliyah game I was talking got me in trouble. This guy had his tongue down my throat so fast, I don't even think I got the word *hello* out.

My curious body and teenage loins soon matched his. We were now in a full make-out session in the car when I realized that time was passing and my mom would be back home pretty soon.

After we exited the car, Mason pinned me up for one last goodbye kiss. Well, what started as a peck turned into a two-minute French kiss, with me leaning between his legs. Then suddenly, I was feeling headlights on the back of my neck.

Then I heard my mother yell, "Emily! Is that you? Oh, I know that's not you!" My mother was completely embarrassed, and going off in front of her church friends.

By now all of the kids that were indoors were now outside, front and center to all of the commotion. My friend looked at me like, *Girl, come on now. How did you get busted?*

My mother didn't say a word to me the entire ride home. Nor that night. Nor the next morning. This definitely had me worried.

♦

After I came home from school the next day, my mother looked at me and said, "We need to talk."

I really wasn't expecting to have "the talk" that afternoon, but in hindsight I guess it was appropriate. She talked to me about him being older than I was, and that she was concerned about him being too mature, blah, blah, blah.

My rebuttal to her was, "But we are in love."

She looked at me with tears in her eyes, walked into her bedroom, and came back to me and said these simple words, "You should really wait to have sex with someone special, but if you must have sex, then use this." She handed me a condom.

I had never seen one before in my life. I thought to myself, *Mom must be on the onset of a breakdown.* I'd never expected those words to come out of her mouth.

After a few weeks passed, Mason officially met my mother. She even approved of us going out on a date or two, even though she'd mentioned that he was too old. I figured by this point she was okay with the idea. Besides, we were in love anyway.

One day, Mason had a bright idea. He suggested that I ditch school for the day to spend the entire day with him, and he'd bring me back before the final bell rang. He told me we were going to hang out with his friend and his girlfriend so we wouldn't be alone. I was game.

The four of us made it to his friend's house, and not too long after arriving, we were off to separate corners, making out, which was now a given every time we saw each other. This time we weren't in public, we were in a house, on a couch, and under a cover, with a mini-fort we'd made to block ourselves from the other couple, who was literally on the other side of the living room in their own mini-fort.

This was the first time I'd ever felt an erect penis. It seemed huge. My heart was literally beating out of my chest. I was sweating and definitely scared to death at what was about to happen. There was no talk or reassurance about whether or not this is what I wanted. It was already assumed that this is what I wanted.

When I felt him fondling my pants—they were white; that's crazy that I remember that—I did stop him to ask if he had a condom, and he did not. Imagine how timely it was for me to have that one single condom in my backpack, the same one my mother had given me a few weeks earlier.

The experience was painful, burned like hell, and seemed to last forever. I wanted to leave, I wanted out, but I was stuck there with him, and of course the other couple, who didn't seem to be finished yet, by the looks of the movement under their mini-fort. We waited for them to finish, and we returned back to school.

Once me and my new ditching home-girl returned to school, I immediately went to the restroom. My insides still burning, I saw hints of blood as I wiped. As soon as the tears were about to come down at the realization of what had just happened, my friend yelled out, "Emily, the dean wants you! Come quick!"

I opened the door to the dean's office and saw my mother's disappointed face. And Aunt Tidy's from Illinois. My heart sank to the floor. I was in big trouble.

I couldn't get my mother's disappointed look out of my head. It was the same look she had when she'd busted me and Mason outside during bible study, the same look she gave me before she went and got the condom out of her room. My aunt and my mother had both come to pick me up from school a bit early to go out to dinner before my aunt headed back to Illinois. When I was nowhere to be found, my mom had decided to wait until I returned.

Before the guilt and shame sank in, I switched it up, telling myself, *Well, the woman said to save my virginity for someone special. Mason* is *special; we're in love.*

As time went on, Mason and I soon became "the perfect couple." We looked great together. Friends from school would tell me how cute we looked together, how gorgeous our children would be. We wore matching outfits and took photos at the local Walmart. We were picture-perfect; I thought we would be together forever. I was on cloud nine.

♦

It was a typical day at school when, sitting in class one day, I received a note on my desk. I looked up and saw this very popular football player staring me right in the face. So I read the note: DO YOU HAVE A BOYFRIEND?

I mouthed the word "Yes." I thought to myself, *Why would he even ask me that? Everyone knows I am Mason's girl.* Besides, he was dating the head cheerleader anyway. Not sure what this dude was thinking. *So random.* I kindly put that foolish note in my back pocket to trash later on.

That evening I went over to Mason's house to spend time with him before going home. After our usual sex session, I went to the restroom to freshen up. When I opened the door to exit, there was Mason, note in hand.

"What the hell is this?" he asked.

I chuckled and started to explain the story to him, but before I could get the words out, he slapped me open-handed, right across the face. I couldn't believe it. I was in utter shock that this man just hit me.

"Don't you ever put your hands on me again!"

"Okay," he said coolly, and then he slapped me dead across the other side of my face.

At this point I had been pimp-slapped not once, but twice. I swear I didn't know what was going on. I didn't know whether or not to scream, run, or call the police. I was shaking, trembling, scared. Mason had a rage in his eyes I had never seen before. Before I knew it, I was not only in tears, but bawling, crying, shaking, on the side of the toilet, curled up, scared for my life.

Then all of a sudden, he was his normal self again. He grabbed my hand, pulled me up from the bathroom floor, and put my head to his chest. He apologized and asked me if I was okay, and of course he wanted to know more about the note. After I explained myself, we made love again, and he took me home. That was the first time he'd hit me, but it definitely wasn't the last. As toxic as our relationship was, Mason and I managed to remain together through a very tough period.

You see, my mother started experiencing breakdowns, and I ended up in foster care. (I can write an entire book just on that journey, and I probably will, so stay tuned). As I dealt with being in and out of the courthouse, and in and out of foster homes, Mason was the only stable factor at the time. At this point, the beatings continued frequently, especially when I questioned him about rumors that he had been sleeping with other girls on the side. I started drinking heavily at this time as well, as a means to numb myself, my emotions, and the hell I was living each day.

I was with Mason for about a year and a half, and was forced to have sex with him on most days, even while on my cycle. I also put up with his drinking binges, fighting, jealous rages, still while appearing to be in love to the outside world. On the back of his car was printed "Mason and Emily forever," and we had both of our names tattooed on our bodies. We were thick as thieves, just the two of us.

I no longer had friends, since he'd stopped that soon after we got together. I recall one time going to the movies with the girls in my foster home. He'd found out somehow and came up to the movies, pulled me out of the theater, and choked me out right there in the entrance of the theater.

As I am gasping for air, with my feet dangling from the ground, I did hear someone mutter, "Man, you shouldn't do her like that," but unfortunately, no one helped.

Mason must have had a friend bring him to the movies, because he dragged me out to someone else's car, pulled me in the back seat, and beat my you know what, while his friend drove. That guy never said a word.

So, yeah, I had no friends, I no longer had my mom, I only had him.

Things started turning around for me once I ended up in a different foster home with a very religious woman. I was the only foster kid there, along with her younger grandson whom she was caring for. She had devotion and prayer every single morning, a full-out Holy Ghost praise party, praising the Lord, playing gospel music, and clapping her hands.

At first it was annoying, but eventually I started paying attention to the Scriptures she was quoting, and the lyrics to the gospel songs she was playing. As time went on, I started to say prayers, very low, almost under my breath during her praise sessions, saying, "Lord, if you hear me, help me get away from this man."

Pretty soon, during our fights, I started hitting back. I started becoming stronger and stronger, seeing visibly that my blows were taking him aback. Then the fights started slowly decreasing, and when they did happen, we were like Ike and Tina (limo scene) by this time, going blow for blow. The roles were reversing. I would have a few scratches; he would have a black eye. I recall choking *him* out one time until he begged for me to stop. I knew right then and there it was just a matter of time before things changed. Maybe God was hearing my prayers. No maybe; He *was*.

♦

A few months later, we had a breakup that seemed to last longer than the usual breakup. Finally, I thought, *This must be it.* Then I found out from a classmate that Mason had started seeing an older woman, and had been for some time.

I remember calling and confronting this woman, and during the conversation, she confessed to seeing him, saying, "It isn't no fun if they don't have anybody."

I figured, *Hey, this is my out. Finally!*

Then weeks later, I got an unexpected call. Mason had tried to kill himself! My heart skipped a beat just at the thought. *Oh no, not again.* My mother had attempted suicide twice while I was in foster care months prior.

I went to see him at the hospital. His family gave me dirty looks, rolling their eyes as I walked in. After I got to his room, he explained that he did this because he didn't want to live anymore if we weren't together. I remember feeling sorry for him. I wanted him to be okay, but the "love" wasn't there anymore. Too much had happened. He had caused me too much pain. I walked out of that hospital room glad that he was alive and well, yet I felt alive myself. I felt free.

His older woman was also there at the hospital, apparently by his side the entire time before I got there. I guess I had caught him while she was on a coffee break. I looked at her, talking crap under her breath to her friend, and just smiled. I thought to myself, *Lady, you can have him.* I walked out of that hospital room and never looked back.

♦ Never lie to try to impress a man; just be yourself, be real.

♦ The "talk" to your children about sex should come much sooner than teenage years and should express your core beliefs (abstinence before marriage, birth control, etc.).

♦ If a man so much as raises his hand to hit you, you beat his behind something fierce with whatever you can get your hand on—iron, skillet, anything.

♦ Being cheated on sucks and should never be tolerated.

♦ With God, you can get out of any toxic relationship, even one involving physical abuse. Just ask Him for strength, for an exit strategy. He will give it to you.

♦ Life goes on. Mason had a whole new girlfriend that next month, my name replaced on the back of his car with hers, his tattoo of my name covered up.

♦ I did successfully learn the signs of a batterer: jealous rages, isolation from friends and family, possessiveness, etc.; and I never dated a batterer again.

♦ Sex isn't love; obsession isn't love; abuse, in all forms, is not love. Know this.

Chapter 20

ALL I DO IS THINK OF YOU

Over time, my stay in Arkansas managed to get better. I was able to move out of foster homes and began to stay with a distant male relative, who worked primarily at night. So, basically, I mainly lived on my own and did whatever I wanted, whenever I wanted.

After my breakup with Mason, my view of men and relationships was somewhat tainted. I didn't feel that sex was special at all; I viewed it as recreational, like a weekend basketball game at the park, or a game of spades at home. It was just something to do, and it didn't seem to hold any significance to anyone. During that time, it seemed like the whole city was having sex outside of their relationship or marriage. Sex being special was BS. I had dated a couple of guys here and there, nothing serious. I was still a heavy drinker, partied a lot on the weekends, and by now had a few consistent friends.

Nonetheless, I did start thinking seriously about college and my future after high school. The more I thought about my future, the more seriously I started taking school at this point. I became more involved with different activities and academic/social clubs at school. I started to notice that there was a group of cool but smart kids who tended to hang together, like a little clique.

I remember having classes with a few of them. I guess this was the first time I came up from my cloud of doom and took notice of them. The guys were well dressed, nice-looking, and seemed pretty smart during class. The girls in the crew were somewhat nice, but considering I was blind to the thought of friends for the past year and a half, I never felt a sense of belonging with them. They had their crew, and that was it. Almost like there was a sign that said "no new friends." I did manage to get close to two other girls, Melissa and Felicia, who took me under their wings, so to speak, and I hung out with them when I could. Although I felt like a "sympathy friend" at times, it was much better than being alone; they served their purpose, a needed purpose, and I was grateful.

One day at school, while getting books out of my locker, I felt someone behind me. I turned around and saw this dude standing there, smiling from ear to ear. So I glanced over to my locker mate, who happened to be a member of the cool/smart crew, and she looked at him looking at me and then proceeded to introduce me to her friend Devin. I remember thinking, *this dude is still smiling ... weird*, and walked away. My first reaction was, this guy is not my type. He's okay-looking, not too pretty, but definitely not ugly. He was dressed nice but seemed way too nice. Like, who sits there and smiles at a girl when they first meet them? How come he wasn't acting cool and aloof like the rest of the guys around school?

After that day, I would see this dude everywhere. In the hallway, still smiling at me, on the bus for a field trip, sitting next to some other chick, but yet still smiling at me.

As time passed, he got more and more interesting. For instance, our school used to have these talent shows in the main auditorium, which I thought was lame most of the time. But this particular year, a set of about five guys danced to something like R. Kelly's "Down Low," and I had to give it to them, these dudes had some moves. Then I started hearing girls screaming as if they were in a concert watching world-famous artists perform.

I looked around thinking, *Are you kidding me? Come on, we are at a high school talent show.* But the more I paid attention, the closer I got to the edge of my seat. There he was, the guy from the locker, the girls around me screaming his name. Now guess who had the goofy grin on her face? I surely did. I was officially intrigued. Heck, damn near a fan.

After that, I couldn't tell you what happened to me. I fell for this guy, and I fell for him hard. I befriended his best friend Derek, making sure he'd relay the message that I was interested in him and to hook it up.

"What's in it for me?" Derek asked, being the jokester he was.

"I'll think of something," I said and passed him my number to give to Devin.

I remember our very first telephone conversation. Devin actually asked me about myself, my likes, my dislikes, what brought me to Arkansas, and the conversation ended without him asking, "When can we hook up?"

Devin was funny, intelligent, ambitious, and very sweet. Overall, he was a handsome young man. My attraction towards him that started off as a 3 was now at a 10! It didn't take long before we were officially dating, and soon after sexually active. I remember him always being responsible, wearing a condom each time. He soon became my "breath of fresh air" during a very rough period of my life, still being away from my immediate family and all. When we were together, nothing else mattered.

In some ways, he was your average teenage boy, and in other ways he was not. For instance, there were times I showed up to parties drunk out of my mind with my friends and would see him across the room. He would smile and walk my way, and as soon as he noticed I was drunk, he would turn the other way. He wouldn't have any dealings with me whenever I was drunk, whereas other guys would take advantage of that situation. Pretty soon Devin was turned off by my behavior and became distant, and eventually we broke up.

Shortly after that, I saw him walking down the school hallway holding hands with some other girl, and you guessed it, he had a smile on his face. He had moved on to the next without skipping a beat. There it was again—the feeling of loss; another person moving on with their life as if I never existed.

The next few months were full of drinking binges, homework, and applying for colleges. Doesn't sound like the best combo, but I felt that I was making some progress and things were moving in the right direction.

I must have had one drinking binge too many because a set of older relatives who just so happened to live across the street had been keeping tabs on me, calling my mother, who now lived back in California, and reporting my behavior to her. How dare they!

The next thing I know, my mom, right in the middle of my senior year, wanted me to return to Los Angeles to live with her. Who does that? I am not sure if I even had a chance to say goodbye to Devin. I remember sitting on that Greyhound bus somewhat excited about finally coming home, yet still I couldn't shake this feeling that I was leaving something behind.

A year later, I graduated from high school, not with honors like I had envisioned months prior, but with a bun in the oven. Yes, I had gotten pregnant by a guy I had been talking to. Our encounter was nothing to brag to your friends about at all. It lasted about a minute, probably less. Matter of fact, it was about three thrusts. Two missed periods later, I was expecting.

Abortion was never an option for me. My immediate thoughts were, *Wow! My very own daughter* (I knew she was a girl), Someone who has no choice but to love me unconditionally, and who will never leave.

I was so delighted, I wrote Devin a letter telling him the good news. We started communicating more often, and eventually that became our thing: writing letters. We did talk on the phone periodically, once to tell me about the passing of a classmate of ours, and again after he got accepted into college. And eventually a call to make plans to come and visit me in LA.

♦

During Devin's visit, we realized that we still had deep feelings for each other. He said, "I want to help you raise Emani." Then he added, "If we hadn't have broken up, you probably wouldn't have been a teen mom. But, don't worry, I'm going to help you get your PhD."

"Really?" A PhD in Psychology was the bright idea I had come up with after graduating from high school, all in an effort to "fix my mom."

"I'll be here for you every step of the way."

Bear in mind, this college freshman could barely manage to pay for his Southwest Airlines flight to come see me. Nonetheless, we tried to make it work. We had a true long-distance relationship for about a year and a half, and saw each other maybe once every five or six months.

Things really started getting rough around the end of my sophomore year. Here I was, in Los Angeles, a very young mother juggling a nine-to-five, taking care of my baby, and going to a local community college in the evening. Devin, on the other hand, was having the ultimate college experience, attending a historically black college in Pine Bluff, Arkansas, where he had pledged to a fraternity. That alone came with unexpected glory and fame, in addition to the typical parties. We were living two totally different lives. Regardless, we were still trying to work it out, believing that we would be together, if it was God's will, though I couldn't help thinking that nothing was going to ever materialize between us.

One day I received a letter in the mail from him. I was all giddy and excited to read it. I remember it like it was yesterday. He wrote: TEMPTATION IS CRAZY OUT HERE IN COLLEGE. THIS GIRL PURSUED ME, AND I COULD ONLY AVOID HER FOR SO LONG. I DON'T THINK I COULD DO THIS.

I called him immediately. After I got over being pissed, I asked for a blow-by-blow account. We decided then to have an open relationship. Well, we knew it was going to be difficult, being two thousand miles away, so if we felt the need to see other people, we would do so, but our foundation, what he and I had, would remain unchanged. He agreed.

I tried dating a little bit, but nothing stuck. All I thought about was Devin, and this broad, whoever she was. I was totally consumed.

He came to visit once more, and I couldn't help being upset about our open relationship (even though it was my idea). I told him that we were getting farther and farther away from the type of love we'd vowed to have for each other, and that he would just have to get his loins under control and suck it up while in school.

He looked me dead in my eyes and said, "I'm sorry, but I just can't do it."

When Devin left for the airport that time around, that was the end of our relationship as we knew it then.

Over the years, he and I kept in touch. He would listen to me as I talked about my relationships, and I would listen to him talk about his. Even though our relationship didn't end like I had hoped, I always appreciated his honesty and that he respected me enough to tell me what he was going through while in college, recognizing that a long-distance relationship wasn't going to work at that point in our lives.

Lessons Learned

♦ I used to wish I'd never moved to Arkansas. Culture shocked yes, but it didn't kill me, I adjusted. Although I had some rough times there, they were all needed for the process. It's part of what makes me, me.

♦ There's nothing wrong with dating the cool/smart guy. Actually, those are the guys you WANT to date. Many of the cute football and basketball players in high school grow up to work at Walmart. Cool/smart guys are in the boardrooms, owning businesses, making that money.

♦ Appreciate an honest man, even though he may not be perfect. I have not once met a man to this day as honest as Devin. So learn to appreciate honesty, even when it's brutal. (This was the first relationship from which I had a clean, no-drama, mutually-agreed-upon breakup.)

♦ Never ever try to hold on to a relationship when it's obvious that it's not working. My grandmother once told me, "If you love someone, let them go. If they come back, great, but if they don't, good riddance."

♦ Open relationships are whack. Not sure who ever came up with that bright idea but they can have it back. My advice? Avoid these types of relationships at all costs.

BEAUTIFUL LIAR

During my open relationship with Devin, I'd met a young man while leaving a nightclub one night with my girls. He ran outside just to get my attention and, of course, asked for my number. I was flattered for a minute, until I turned around to enter the parking elevator. I could've sworn I saw that same guy, run out of those same club doors again, all to get some other girl's attention. I thought to myself, *That bastard! That must be his MO.*

Nonetheless, when Mike did finally call several weeks later, his timing was perfect, considering Devin had just written me his "college confessions" letter. We talked on the phone for hours, as if I had known him for years.

Mike ended the conversation, saying, "Well, I gotta go hop in the shower. Getting ready to come pick you up for the movies. See you in an hour."

I paused for a second, looked at my phone, and was immediately tickled. "See you in an hour."

During our first date, I had told Mike that I was dating someone out of state, and he was perfectly fine with that. He didn't try to push up on me or anything; he was more like a predator waiting patiently for its prey.

Once Devin and I broke up officially, Mike was the perfect rebound. He was right there with a shoulder to cry on, ready to take me out for dinner and drinks to take my mind off things, and to come up to my apartment afterward and make things all better with that good ol' *D*.

Our time together at first was strictly physical. Having just gotten out of a relationship, I had convinced myself that I wasn't ready for another one. And Mike was totally fine with not having anything official and to just "see where things would lead."

One thing I admired about Mike was that he was a dad. I knew he had a daughter slightly older than mine, at this time two and a half going on three, but it didn't dawn on me until he finally met my daughter that he was definitely a natural. Without skipping a beat, he strapped her in the booster seat and helped her with her dinner.

On my daughter's third birthday party, he brought his daughter, Monica to meet us both. She was a sweet little girl, well-mannered, and the two of them looked very cute together. That day, seeing the two of them, I imagined the four of us together as a family.

As the months progressed, Mike played his part, taking the girls to the park, movies, and the beach, and with sleepovers. By this time, I was about to turn twenty-one, and we had been dating for about two years. Then we started having the "where-are-we-going-from-here" discussions, and his excuses were all centered around my shortcomings.

"Your attitude is too bad," he said one night when we were having a talk.

I looked him dead in the eye. "Is that why I've never met your daughter's mother or any of your family or friends?"

"You act too jealous."

"Funny you should say that," I said, shaking my head from side to side, "with all the times you don't answer your phone, or leave my house abruptly. You think I haven't noticed the strange behavior?"

"You nag me too much, man. Gotdamn! Why is everything a problem?"

I knew deep down something was up with this dude, but I just couldn't put my finger on it.

I started going through his cell phone looking for frequent calls. Nothing. Through his pants pockets for numbers. Nothing.

But then one day he was supposed to come by, and it appeared he was going to be a no-show, which was unusual for him. About an hour had passed, and he finally called me to tell me his car had been stolen from Fox Hills Mall. I asked him if he wanted me to come up there to get him, and he said no, that he was all right and would get a ride to my house and stop by for a minute.

He did what he said, stopped by, told me what had happened, made a quick phone call to have someone pick him up. Something about that night just didn't seem right. I sat on my couch in dead silence. Then I thought, *He made a phone call—a perfect time for good ol' star sixty-nine.*

"Good evening. Thank you for calling Bakers. Lauren speaking."

I hung up, my heart racing. *Who in the heck is Lauren?*

I waited until the following morning and called the number again. Another person answered the phone.

I asked, "What Bakers is this?"

She said, "Fox Hills Mall."

"Thank you."

Hmmm, a clue to my investigation, his car was stolen at that same mall, but I still needed to know who this Lauren was.

That weekend, Mike and I had planned an outing with the girls, so I convinced him to leave his daughter with mine while he went to go play basketball. The deal was, I would have them that morning, and he would take them later in the afternoon so I could attend a wedding.

So that morning, Monica came over, and the plan was to simply spark up conversation, and perhaps I could get more info about the mystery girl. I know it wasn't cool to use the kids, but at this point, I was desperate.

As she rode a little play tricycle through the house, yapping away about this and that, I asked her, "You know anyone named Lauren?"

"Sure, I do! That's my dad's friend."

"Oh really? Your dad's friend? I take it you've met her before."

"Of course!" she said. "She spends the night at my dad's house all the time.'

By this time my heart was pumping and my palms were sweating. I was fuming! I pulled myself together, to not expose myself in front of his daughter or mine, put their shoes on, and loaded them in the car. We were off to the mall, to Bakers.

As we walked up to the store, my heart was beating extremely fast. I didn't know what to expect. This was such a bold move, but something was still pulling me there. I had to know. *This must be the chick hindering us from moving forward,* I thought. I just needed to know who she was, so I went in for the kill.

I walked through the door, with one girl on each hand, and instantly, Monica released my hand and ran up to the clerk behind the counter squealing, "Lauren! Lauren!"

Lauren kneeled down and greeted her. "Oh wow! Who are you here with, sweetie? Are you here with your mom?"

Now hovering over her, I looked down at Lauren with the most stank look on my face. "No, she's with me." I started looking around the store, pretending to be interested in shoes, trying to catch my breath so I could at least carry out what I came here for.

I thought to myself, *What the heck! Might as well get some real help. I really do need some shoes for the wedding.* So, I asked her to run to the back and get me a few pairs, all the while trying to figure out what to say to her.

As she was ringing me up, I finally mustered the nerve to say, "Hey, I came here because I've been seeing a guy for the past two years. He called you from my house, and I simply want to know—how do you know Mike?"

"Mike? Mike is my boyfriend; we've been together for three and a half years."

Her response was the last thing I'd expected. I felt like I had been hit by a dump truck. I thought I was about to go confront some woman about my man, only to find out that I was confronting someone about *hers*.

We exchanged numbers, and she promised to call after her shift. We both swore not to talk to Mike until the two of us talked. I went to drop the girls off to Mike and didn't say a word. Then I attended my friend's wedding, the details of which I barely remember.

I was glad when I finally did receive the call from Lauren. We met up that evening at a local restaurant to discuss things. I had my friend Giovanna with me, and she had two of her girls. When I saw her the second time, it was a little weird how similar we were—same height and build, same complexion, same length hair—okay, mine was a weave, but hey—similar features, even down to the same color car.

One of Lauren's friends said, "Mike practically has two versions of the same girl."

Everyone laughed.

We sat and compared notes. Details like, whose house did he go over for Thanksgiving months prior? Funny thing, he had made both, early for her dinner and late for mine. Generally speaking, when he was MIA with me, he was with her.

Before the night was over, we had plotted to flush him out. They would meet me back at my apartment to hide, and when he came to drop off the girls, we would bust him.

Lauren and her friends actually hid out at Giovanna's apartment, which was in the same complex, downstairs from mine. When Mike called to say he was on his way, we were all in position. After he came upstairs with our daughters, Lauren would soon follow.

Well, when Mike came, things didn't go as planned. He came with only my daughter, politely placed her in my house, and then turned back around and went outside. He paused at the top of the stairwell and yelled through the apartment courtyard, "Lauren, you can come out!"

How did he know he was being ambushed?

Lauren came from downstairs, and there we were, the three of us, for a short moment of silence. Just as I began to think we were going to go inside, sit down, and confront him, he turned from the both of us and started walking away, toward the front entrance of the apartment.

I said, "So you just not going to say anything to us, asshole?"

Lauren then said, "So you're just going to walk away from me?"

We both walked behind him trying to keep up with his brisk walk as he pled the Fifth. He made it all the way outside and got in his car and closed the door.

That just pissed me off. As he drove off, I kicked the mess out the side of his car. He skirted off, just shaking his head at my dramatic gesture.

As Lauren and I both stood in the middle of the street, watching him turn the corner, I said, "Sorry about that. I was a little pissed."

"No, that was really good, actually."

We both laughed. We met our friends at the apartment entrance, and we parted ways.

After I went upstairs, and put my daughter to bed, my girlfriend called me soon after.

"Have you cried yet?" she asked.

I responded, "No, not yet. Crazy night, huh," and we said our goodbyes.

The moment I hung up the phone, the tears immediately flowed nonstop.

The next morning was a Sunday. I didn't eat anything. My middle sister, Aretha called. I told her about the drama. I then ran some errands.

I walked around all day like a zombie. I just couldn't believe it. I had spent the last two years with a guy, trying to figure out the reasons why he possibly wouldn't commit to me fully, walking around thinking something is wrong with me, only to find out that he had been living a double life this whole time.

I thought about his daughter, how confused she must be, to spend days and nights over here with us, and then turn around and spend time yet with another woman. To say the least, I felt the utmost betrayal. He didn't even have the audacity to explain himself to me, to her, to no one. He just got in his car and left. WOW! What balls this man had!

I also started reflecting on the conversation I'd had the prior night with Lauren. She'd brought pictures of them to our little pow-wow, told stories about birthday parties she had thrown for him. Where all of his friends attended. The friends that I'd heard of but never had the pleasure of meeting. It really started to sink in that I was officially "the other woman," or "side-piece."

By Sunday night, I started feeling a little better. I think I even changed my cell number at that point.

My girlfriend called on the house phone and asked, "Have you heard from him?"

"Not a peep."

I went to bed that night still a bit confused as to what was going on. *Could it be that the guy I spent nearly two years of my life with is a complete fraud?* Although part of me wanted to just walk away from it all and never look back, I also wanted answers. I needed to speak with Mike and hear this for myself. I wanted to know the truth, even if it hurt. I decided to wait until things died down and hopefully he would call.

The next morning, as I was getting ready for work, I heard the phone ring. My first thought was, *It's Mike. He's the only one that would call this early.* I looked at the caller ID. *He's finally calling.* I answered the phone with the most stank attitude. "What do you want, Mike?"

"This isn't Mike, it's Lauren."

My heart sank yet again. This time it fell out of my chest cavity and directly onto the floor.

"I just wanted to call and tell you that Mike and I talked, and we've decided to work things out."

My response was cool and nonchalant, of course. "I wish you the best, and thanks for letting me know. I just have one question—when did he call you? Or did you have to call him?"

"He called me immediately after we left your house and begged me to come over. I've been over here ever since."

Right then and there, that should have been all I needed to walk away. The guy I had been with the last two years was a fraud, living a complete double life the entire time we'd been together. Honestly, I wasn't even sure that I was number two. I always had a feeling that the baby's mother was still around, in the picture somehow. Who's to say that he didn't have more women out there?

Well, I didn't let go. I had to hear Mike's side of the story. I had to know that I just wasn't sloppy seconds, that somewhere, somehow, the time spent with him wasn't in vain. That having someone that close to my daughter wasn't in vain. That getting to know someone else's daughter and treating her as if she were my own wasn't in vain. I needed answers. I had to hear from him.

A few days later, I mustered up enough nerve to call Mike, with my brand-new cell phone number, giving it away. I asked if he was with Lauren, and he said "yes", in a very cocky and arrogant tone. I told him to call me back when he had the chance, and that it was important that I speak with him.

The next day he gave me a call. This time, he wasn't so arrogant. He chose to be apologetic and went a little left with the conversation. He started to tell me how they'd met, other personal details I don't even feel comfortable mentioning, since that's her story that he shouldn't have even told, basically, trying to discredit this girl's character.

I thought, *Wait a minute—This is the girl you have chosen. Why do you feel it's necessary to slander her?* You *are the* A-*hole here, not her.* I knew better than to fall for this okie-doke.

He did mention something that stood out to me. He said, "I am with her because I know she will never leave me. You, on the other hand, I wonder if you are going to leave me by the day. You don't take my shit. I know if I messed up, you would leave in a heartbeat. And I can't promise you I won't mess up; I am not perfect."

For whatever reason, that statement messed me up for the next several days. I wondered if I had been going about this whole relationship stuff all wrong. Should I not be so black or white? Should I spend more time showing men that I will be there for them through thick and thin? I needed to know more about this approach to dating. *Why not hear it from the source?* I thought. So I gave Lauren a call and asked if we could hook up for dinner.

We met, this time alone, and talked over dinner. We traded more stories about our history with Mike, and it became evident that we had been sharing a man this entire time. We weren't sure how he had the balls, time, or even the energy to do it all. From family time, to date nights, to holidays, he managed to spend just enough time with the both of us to not raise too much suspicion.

Eventually we started talking about each other's sex life. I had been pressing to get that out of her because the brotha had a very strong sex drive. Wore me out on most days. So I couldn't fathom how he had someone else, and wondered if things were slower on their end. Nope, the same. And the same thought had occurred to her.

We also discovered that he rarely used condoms with both of us, and neither of us was on birth control. The similarities were striking and sad.

After dinner that night, we talked a few more times on the phone, even shared a few laughs. We also met up another time at a mall and did some shopping. What seemed to be some simple "girlfriend time" was two women talking about being betrayed by the same man.

I must admit, our continued interaction was therapeutic. No judgment was cast, because both of us had been dealing with the same man and his foolishness, so in a sense it was a way to talk things out with a person who could truly empathize with my situation, having been through the same drama.

Over the next several weeks to a month of meeting and talking with Lauren, I hid from her the whole time I was still talking with Mike. I remember the day we'd come from the mall, he'd left a note for me, a poem actually, talking about I was his rib, that he couldn't live without me, blah, blah, blah. I crumpled it up, not really falling for it. To me, my ultimate revenge was befriending his girlfriend. But there was a twist—he didn't know I was talking to Lauren, and she didn't know I was still talking to him.

"Love triangle" was what my friend Lanita called it, after she'd called me up and I filled her in on all the details of my drama.

She asked me, "What is this girl like?"

"She's actually a nice person, very pretty, funny, and she could sing. I could totally see why Mike is with her. She's great. Had we met any other time, outside of Mike, we probably would be close friends, like BFFs."

"Like BFFs, huh?"

"Yes, like BFFs."

I told her that we both felt the same connection, and would joke that we would stay friends for life, and that she plans to bust in singing "The Upper Room" at my funeral (from the movie *Life*).

My friend didn't find any humor in what I was saying at all. She went in on me immediately.

"You are falling in love with this girl—you are in a love triangle!"

I was like, "What the hell—What do you mean? I am not gay!"

"Okay, not like that, but you are definitely getting caught up way too deep. This girl is not your friend; she is your man's girlfriend. Does that even make sense? No! So why are you acting like this girl is your friend? Stop talking to her *now*. And definitely stop talking to him!"

I wish I had listened to her.

To make a long story short, this sort of love triangle went on for a few more months, which was very taxing emotionally. Eventually Lauren and I both learned that he was still sleeping with us both from time to time.

Then things turned ugly fast. Especially when I heard the words "How could you sleep with him?" come out of her mouth, when I was getting ready to say the same damn thing. Enough was enough. He was not going to stop, she was not going to stop. It was just time to move on.

I finally got the courage to let go of Mike. Actually, both of them.

♦ Take time to heal after a breakup. Rebounds usually don't ever work out.

♦ If you feel deep down that something is not right, it probably isn't! Pay attention to the red flags.

♦ Once you find out he is cheating, leave him. Like, immediately! A relationship built on lies and deception is just too toxic. Sharing a man simply sucks. Never, ever, ever, ever should you put up with a man who you know is seeing someone else. You deserve better. And there are plenty of available men out there.

♦ One of the number one tactics of a cheating man is to discredit his other woman. Don't fall for this. There is something keeping him from leaving her, and that should be enough to fuel you to leave him.

♦ Don't waste time trying to win a man's heart, especially if you are in direct competition with someone else. This is a no-win situation. Even after you think you've won, it's only a matter of time until someone else comes along and takes your position as the other woman. It's inevitable.

♦ The other woman is not the enemy (or your friend), *he* is. Let him go.

Chapter 4
UPGRADE YOU

It had been about a year or so since my love triangle had finally fizzled out. I was single, dating different guys here and there. Nothing to write home about. I had also begun going to church more frequently, reading a lot of self-help relationship books, desperate not to make the same mistakes I had made previously. I had started a new job in the Business Department at Cedars-Sinai Medical Center, one of the better-known hospitals in Beverly Hills, CA, where all of Hollywood goes to receive care. Upon my first days there, I noticed that there were several other very beautiful women working in my department. Having come from working at a job where I was the only black girl, and so happened to be good-looking at that, there was no competition. Now, at this place, I had to figure out where I would fit in, because these girls were gorgeous. Young, successful, and free. At least that's how they appeared to be externally. Dressed to impressed, hair done, nails done, everything done. I knew I had to step up my game to fit in this place. No more wearing the same outfits or raggedy flats every day.

As time went on, I befriended these pretty girls very quickly. Hey, if you can't beat them, join them, right? In hindsight, these women, who were maybe just a few years older than I, subtly introduced me to a totally different desire and a taste for a potential mate. My new friends were in various types of relationships. Two of my new coworker friends were married, and their husbands tended to spoil them with the latest handbags, nice trips, mini shopping sprees, and kept them driving the latest luxury vehicles. Another had a hustler for a baby daddy, a foreigner, who must have been treating her well, by the clothes she wore and her flawless hair. Lastly, there was this woman who let it be known that she dated multiple men at a time, none of whom earned less than a six-figure salary. They would wine and dine her, give her money to splurge with, and take her on exotic trips, all of which were definitely foreign to little ol' me. I was used to the movies and maybe dinner after, definitely not three-thousand-dollar checks with "Enjoy yourself" in the memo.

Don't get me wrong, I had a few encounters in my day with men that had money. For some reason, one of my best friends, Stacy, had a knack for picking up men with money. It was like a rare gift. And she wasn't flashy like the women at my new job. She was simply down-to-earth, had a great sense of humor, and said exactly what she thought at all times. Men were attracted to her physically but probably more so to her personality. She was as real as they get, and I can only presume that men with money appreciated that in her.

Well, once Stacy got married, she then diverted all of these men my way. Lucky me! All in about six months, she had introduced me to three professional athletes.

One baseball player's opening line was, "I am engaged and play for the San Diego Padres. But I would love for you to be 'my girl' when I am in Los Angeles.'"

"Um, no thanks!" That was the last I heard of him.

Second guy was a player on the Los Angeles Lakers. We

were invited to a club with him and some of the other players on the team. Just standing beside them, my eye leveled slightly above their belt buckle (I'm only five two) was a turn-off to me, so I quickly decided that wouldn't work, just because the height difference scared me.

Lastly, with another baseball player, we managed to make it past the second date. On that second date, he decided to tell me he was married, but that wouldn't interfere with what "we had."

Great. Just great. I asked to be taken home.

He insisted on walking me upstairs. He took a quick look at my apartment, and my pleather couch. "You live here? You and your daughter?"

I told him, "Yes," feeling slightly insulted. "I'm doing the best I can."

He pulled out his money clip and quickly gave me ten hundred-dollar bills. He said that if that wasn't enough, he could go to the ATM and get more. I told him that was fine (even though I was screaming inside). I also told him I was tired and needed to go pick up my daughter before it got too late, and that he had to go. I thanked him for the date, and the money, and never answered his calls after that.

Fast-forward to my new friends who seemed to have dating men with money all figured out. For months, I lived vicariously through these women. My Coach bags weren't good enough anymore. I wanted Prada and Gucci. No more shoe-shopping at Bakers for me. I had moved up to Aldo, Macy's, and Nordstrom. I bought new suits and work attire from Express (using my newly approved credit card, of course), and even bought better hair for my extensions. I had officially stepped my game up, and wanted a new man to match my new fly appearance.

One Sunday morning, after the sermon, a slightly older, but polite man stopped me and my daughter, who was about five at the time. First glance, he was decent-looking, but had he not stopped us, I probably would have walked past him without noticing. He began to say how he admired the dynamic between my daughter and I during service (she'd always been very affectionate), and he just wanted the pleasure to meet us and tell us how he enjoyed watching us from afar.

My daughter and I looked at each other.

I said, "Oookkaaayyyy."

He then told my daughter he had tickets to a Nickelodeon event and asked if she would like to go.

Of course, she squealed, "Yes, Mommy, yes!"

Then he said, "Well, I would need your mom's phone number so I can get her the tickets. Mom, what do you say?"

I gave him the side eye with a quick smirk. *This dude thinks he's slick.* However, I went ahead and gave him my number. He got an A for effort.

It didn't take long before Dean had my undivided attention. He was a charming guy with a heck of a past. He was pretty transparent about his life, giving me all the details over the phone before he even asked me out. This guy had recently come out of prison, maybe had been home for two months or so. Had served time in the federal penitentiary and owed several major corporations restitution for hacking into their systems and stealing classified data. He had even written a book about it.

Okay, I know it sounds scary, but on a positive note, he was a single dad with two sons, and I was definitely convinced by his personality and great sense of humor that he was home for good and didn't want anything else but to make an honest living, and to get on his feet the right way.

Our first date was at a Lakers game, my first Lakers game actually, with fantastic seats. We had dinner another night, and the next day he surprised me at my job on my lunch break. I immediately thought, *Oh, this is great! I can introduce him to my girls and see what they think about him.*

So we all gathered around, downstairs at the mini café in front of our building while he name-dropped all the celebrities he knew, what business ventures he had in the works, and on and on.

My coworker friends were more than impressed. Once he drove off in his Lexus, one of them turned to me and said, "Oh, Emily, he's fantastic! He's the one!" I think we all even had a group hug after that. Go figure.

While I was on the way to his sky-rise apartment in Marina Del Rey later that week, I couldn't help but wonder what to expect. The guy said he was getting on his feet, but living in an apartment with a doorman greeting me is not what comes to mind when someone says they are getting on their feet.

He welcomed me at the door, and I walked in to the most gorgeous view of the city of Los Angeles I had ever seen. I was sure I couldn't hide the look on my face. His place was beautiful. I was convinced I wanted this life. I wanted to lock him in, ex-con or not. I believed in him and wanted a piece of this life that he so frequently offered me and my daughter.

The next several months were great. We went to church together. I met his sons; all five of us would spend a lot of time together. I immediately went into "mommy mode," trying to prove that even though he was eleven years older, I could do the job of being a mother to his sons, and be a great wife. At twenty-three, that was my mission.

I cooked for them, got groceries, all while Dean was "getting on his feet." He worked late nights, had several business meetings, but still had time to take me to new restaurants, and host me and my friends at his place for drinks, dinner, and casual fun. He even hosted Christmas dinner at his house for me and my family. He presented me with several gifts, all wrapped individually, at least ten gifts. From small trinkets to larger gifts, to a grand finale. The presentation was oh-so-clever and cute.

He showered my daughter with gifts as well. Both parents, my sister, even my 98-year-old grandmother left that day highly impressed by this guy.

A few months later Dean hosted my twenty-fourth birthday party at his apartment with a host of our family and friends. At this point we were about six months into the relationship. On my actual birthday a few days later, he surprised me at work for lunch, took me to Crustacean restaurant in Beverly Hills, bought me a Tiffany necklace and bracelet, my very first Louis Vuitton bag and a pair of Charles David boots. He spent close to two grand just on my lunch break alone. I was so happy at this point, I couldn't wait to go into the office and show off my goodies to my friends. I remember they came by one by one to my cubicle, jaws dropping, in complete awe. Finally, I had earned my way into the club.

Well, a week later, it was Valentine's Day weekend as well as the NBA's All-Star weekend here in Los Angeles. I noticed that he was pretty distant, so I automatically thought that I was in for a big surprise for Valentine's Day. I wondered how he would top my birthday and what he had up his sleeve.

The day before Valentine's Day, we had the biggest argument. Over what, I don't even remember. He mentioned that he would have out-of-town guests for the weekend and may be "tied up." I spent Valentine's Day all alone, pissed off to the max. I didn't hear from him at all that day. Wasn't talking to him the next day or the day after.

I went into work the following Monday, and all my coworkers were asking what Dean had done for me for our very first Valentine's Day. I didn't even lie to them. I told them that he was MIA and that we weren't speaking at the moment. They just quietly turned around and walked away with raised eyebrows.

He tried to make up for that disastrous weekend with some lame excuse about how he was hosting business clients, and time escaped him. That was my first major red flag. However, I forgave him.

As time went on, he started making more money, and moved from Marina Del Rey to a beautiful beach home a few blocks away from Venice Beach. I thought he would have asked for me and my daughter to move in with him, but he did not. It was just enough bedrooms for him and his boys. My daughter and I were there quite often, but as things picked up financially for him, things started to go downhill for us.

He had given me a key to his house, and one afternoon I got off early from work and stopped by before picking up my daughter from school. I found the house empty, and the kitchen a mess, as if someone had just cooked lunch. I saw two sets of plate ware, and two wine glasses, one with lipstick on it. I simply cleaned up and didn't bring it up.

Other times I would visit him at the office and tell the front desk receptionist that I was there to see him. They would ask who I was, and I would politely say, "Tell him his girlfriend Emily is here to see him." Of course, every time I received the same reaction, with stuttering and throat clearing.

"Okay, ma'am, I'll tell Mr. Williams you're here."

Dean would often call me to his office to pick up a check.

Our agreement was that he would give me a check for $2500 every time he made a deal. The deals went from once a month to every two weeks, to sometimes once a week. Every time, I would be right there at that office picking up my check. Eventually, I started seeing other women in the office, coming and going, around the same time I was. They would have the same envelope in their hand as I did. I confronted him about it, and of course he got all defensive and obnoxious, so I never mentioned it again.

Then I started noticing other strange behavior. I would come by unannounced and find him talking ever so gently to someone on the phone, sometimes with his hand down his pants. I would bust right on in the room, and he would quickly hang up the phone, straighten up, and act as if nothing happened. Another time, I caught him arguing with one of his "employees" where they would get loud, he'd hang up, and keep dialing the number back again and again, basically blowing this employee's phone up. I thought it had to been a female because no man usually blows up another man's phone, period. And if it was a female, she wasn't an employee.

And these weren't the only incidents. I knew deep down inside that Dean was seeing other women. This time, things were a little different. Everyone knew I was his girl, from his friends, his family, his lawyers to his colleagues. Now whether or not I was his only one was a different story. Was I okay now that I was the main chick, and not the side-chick like in the previous relationship? Was I okay because I benefited from this relationship financially? Perhaps since the relationship was moving so fast, and things were changing so fast, I didn't have time to catch my breath. I didn't start feeling like I wanted out until month nine.

I recall Dean telling me one evening that he was going to play pool with the guys. Usually, this wouldn't be a big deal at all; we went our separate ways on many occasions. One thing I liked about him having time with his boys and me with my girls is that he'd drop me a few hundred dollars for the night for me and my girls to enjoy ourselves. This particular evening, I was at my own apartment when he told me he was going out. Something didn't seem right.

I called my best friend Stacy and told her something was fishy.

"Do we need to go do a drive-by?" she asked.

I said, "We sure do. Let's go!"

I picked up my sister, Aretha along the way as well, and the three of us headed out to Venice.

When I arrived at his house, his car was missing, but I knew that that didn't mean a thing. I had recently had my key revoked from all of my pop-up visits, so I had to remember where he kept the spare key. *In the flower vase outside the back door!* Yes, it was still there.

I entered the house. I yelled out to see if anyone was home, but there was no response. However, I did hear music playing. I followed the music and saw that the lights were dim in the den area, the fireplace crackling. Candles were out but not lit, and a bottle of wine was sitting on ice. I thought to myself, *Hmmm. Maybe they had just left.*

I went back out to the car, where my best friend and sister were waiting, and they asked if I was ready to go.

I told them, "No. This gonna be a long night. I'm waiting for these fools to get back."

We waited for over forty-five minutes before we saw lights come down the narrow street. Sure enough, we saw a car pull into the garage. Not his car though.

Just in the nick of time, Stacy and I jumped out the car and ran under the garage door right before it closed. We scared the mess out of Dean and his lady friend.

Dean yelled, "What the heck is going on? Why are you here?"

He blabbered some other crap, but whatever he was saying was literally going through one ear and out the other. I couldn't take my eyes off the female he was with. This one didn't look anything like me. She was short, very petite, and dark-complexioned with long hair. Nonetheless, I must give it to her—she was beautiful.

Despite Dean's tirade and Stacy talking trash right back at him, the girl and I were completely calm.

I finally opened my mouth and said to the young lady, "Excuse me, are you on a date right now?"

Dean intervened, "No, we aren't on a date, and if we were, it's none of your business."

I asked her again, "Sweetie, are you two on a date?"

She responded, "Yes, we are!"

"Thank you."

The woman gained my utmost respect at that very moment. No drama, no attitude, no lashing out. Woman to woman, she let it be known that my man was being unfaithful.

I stormed upstairs, grabbed a piece of luggage, and started gathering all of my belongings. He ran upstairs after me, explaining that she was nothing, that his homeboy tried to hook him up with her, he didn't even have her number, and that he'd entertained her as a courtesy.

After completely ignoring every word coming from his mouth, I was out of there. I threw the bag in the car, my sister and best friend stunned at the night's events, and I wept the entire ride home.

And cried myself to sleep once I got there.

I wish I could tell you that was the end of my story with Dean, but there is more. About a week or so had passed, and I wasn't accepting Dean's calls, though he was sending flowers to the job by the dozens. I had just picked up my daughter from school and was driving down the street.

My daughter screamed, "Mommy, Mommy, there's Mike!"

I rolled down my window, and glanced at the next car over. There he was, my raggedy ex, my daughter so happy to see him.

He yelled, "Hi, Emani. How are you? I miss you!"

"I miss you, too" as she glanced in his back seat, obviously looking for Monica, his daughter.

While we were still stuck in traffic, he asked, "Can we plan a play date, for just the girls?"

"Sure. Just call me."

Mike called and arranged a play date for the girls for that very weekend. When he picked her up from the house, and I saw the girls immediately hug and start to play, I had a warm, fuzzy feeling inside. These girls had literally grown up as sisters, and it was so unfair that it had to end because of his indiscretions. It couldn't be anything wrong with them getting together from time to time, could it?

♦

Mike brought the girls back a few hours later. They came in the house and ran straight to Emani's room. Then there we were, just me and him. I no longer had any butterflies, or felt any type of way. Besides, I was going through my own drama at the time.

He asked how I was and if I was dating. Of course I told him yes, and that I was happy in another relationship (I lied) and in turn asked how was he. He responded, saying he was dating too, and things were cool.

So I thought that was odd for him to say he was "dating." So I asked, "Are you still with Lauren?"

"Yes, I still see her, but I'm not faithful to her."

Same ole, same ole raggedy dog. Although I must admit, deep down, there was some sense of satisfaction. I think I almost grinned. *He's the same even without me being in the picture.* Maybe they weren't meant to be, after all. Mike left shortly after that. Our first encounter since the end of our love triangle went a lot smoother than I thought it would.

♦

A few weeks had gone by, and Dean was trying desperately to get back with me, laying it on thick, I must say.

Something about that evening of our stakeout still had me very uneasy. *Humph,* I thought, *he didn't even have her number. I'm sure that was a lie.* I recall having access to his cell phone bill. I wanted to see if I could go back to that night, just to see what I could find. I looked up the date and time we were there on our stakeout, and saw several calls to the same number shortly after we had left.

I called that number, and sure enough, I got the voice mail of the girl he'd been on a date with. I remembered her name because he'd said it during our encounter in the garage. So he lied. Lied right to my face. He did have her number, and he did call her that night. This scene was oh-too-familiar for me, and the feeling I had made me extremely sad.

I didn't have my daughter that night and was home alone sulking in my new findings. I took a ride to the liquor store and got a bottle of Hennessy, my favorite during times like this.

I remember calling my favorite male cousin, Kelvin. He was hot stuff on top of being an ex-professional ball player. My friends were forever asking about him, although he was now married with kids. *I'm sure Kelvin will tell me the real.* Slurred speech and all, I told him all of what happened and simply asked him, "Cuz, do all men cheat? Is this something that I just have to get used to? Please, tell me the truth."

"No, Em, all men do NOT cheat. You will just have to let this one go and wait for God to send you someone that doesn't."

That pep talk lasted for all of about fifteen minutes. The liquor was in full effect. I was officially drunk, depressed, crying, the whole nine.

I decided to take a shower, hoping to sober up a bit. I put on a cute tight-fitting dress and makeup, not sure where I was going. I just wanted to look and feel better.

I remember getting my bible out, with liquor in my glass, and saying out loud, very loud actually, "Okay, Em, you can trust God, read this Bible, pray and take your drunk ass to bed, or you can call someone to get you over this hump."

I had just had a conversation with my sister early that day about how easy it is to get over one man with another man, thus the latter part of my conflicting decision. Well, you guessed it, I picked option #2.

I put the bible down, guzzled down the last of my drink, picked up the phone and called Mike. He was at my house within five minutes. He asked if I was okay and what was going on. I told him my boyfriend cheated, he's a jerk, and that I missed *us.*

I didn't have to say anything else. A round of hot, passionate, get-back-at-your-ex-with-another-man sex soon followed. He called me beautiful, like he used to say so many times when we were together. He also complimented me on my body, which was twenty pounds lighter than when we were together. He was saying all the right things, laying the game on thick, talking about he missed us, and he missed this, how could he have let me go before. You know the drill.

The next morning, I woke up on the couch alone, my revenge strategy leaving me hungover and confused. I didn't feel any better at all; I had just complicated things tenfold.

♦

I eventually gave Dean another chance. He had always had the gift of gab, which I guess I wasn't able to resist. Besides, things were going so well with his business, he basically bought my way back into his life. We took trips, and I got everything I asked for: new clothes, jewelry, Apple computers, even a new Mercedes-Benz. I still didn't trust him fully and wasn't willing to give him my all again. So I continued to sleep with Mike on the side, as a means to protect my heart.

This was the first time ever that I not only dated two men at the same time but slept with two men simultaneously. I knew what I was doing was wrong, but I just didn't care anymore. I was out to get mine, just like these men are usually out to get theirs.

Mike was in heaven because I was too busy watching my own back to even remotely worry about what he was doing. This lasted only about two months before my relationship with Dean came to an end from the constant arguing. I couldn't get over the mistrust, and deflecting my own indiscretions back on to Dean probably wasn't helping either.

Boy, was my breakup with Dean crazy. First, he tried every get-her-back strategy he could think of, including sending packages of $500 up to my job with a note saying, have fun with your girls this weekend. I would give the package right back to the delivery person who'd bring it up there.

One night he popped up over my house, and Mike was there. He was banging on the door, and I eventually had to call the police. Having another man at the house only pissed him off, and he took things to a whole new level.

A few days later, after I arrived at work, my cell phone started blowing up. It was one of my coworker friends (of the fabulous crew) telling me that Dean had called her and repeated back to her all the gossip I had told him about her, saying that I wasn't a good friend, and that I was running around town with my ex, in the car he bought. I hung up the phone with that friend. *WOW, the nerve of him!*

The next moment, my other home girl came strutting down the hallway to my cubicle with a note in her hand, saying Dean had left it on her car: URGENT. PLEASE CALL.

"What's this about?" she asked.

I told her, "Please ignore it. He's pissed that we broke up and that I have been seeing someone else. Do not respond!"

Sure enough, another one of my friends came to my cubicle with tears in her eyes. Dean had called and told her that he knew about the baby she had recently lost, and that she had taken it extremely hard, but her boyfriend was not as understanding, almost relieved in a sense. I know that was a very sensitive topic for her. I'd told him during pillow talk that I was concerned about her being depressed.

To show you how great of a person she was, instead of going off on me as I thought she would have, she gave me a big hug, tears still running down her face, and told me she was so sorry that I was going through this, and that she forgave me.

I really needed that hug.

As soon as I thought things were okay, my friend, the one who I'd told not to call Dean, came strutting down the hall and busted in my cubicle. She looked me dead in the eye. "Did you really tell him that I am a brown-noser to our boss, and that all I do is date men with money and will never date anyone who is broke?"

Now at this point I wanted to say, "Well, all of that is true. Not sure why you're upset." But I couldn't, given the circumstances. All I could do was apologize. That friend was not as forgiving. We took years to heal from that incident.

Needless to say, there were a few other friends Dean had reached out to. Every single detail I had ever discussed with him during pillow talk, simple talk, or gossip about my friends was repeated to them. I was humiliated. If his goal was to hurt me, it worked.

In hindsight, his whole retaliation efforts were the driving force behind me leaving him and never looking back. I ignored all of his phone calls, text messages, returned all gifts, etc. This went on for weeks, actually months. From anger retaliation, to drastic measures wanting me back. I stayed strong, I did not waiver. Eventually, it was the end of the best and the worst relationship I had had thus far.

♦ Don't be blinded by money when dating a high-profile, high-income earner. Red flags are red flags.

♦ Never stay in a relationship because of financial security. It's best to make your own money anyway. Be your own boss!

♦ Skip the pillow talk and keep your girlfriends' business to yourself. Better yet, get a hold on gossip altogether. It's just not cool and better not done in the first place.

♦ Be the person that you want in a relationship. If you want trust, be trustworthy. If you want faithfulness, be faithful. Honesty, be honest. It's never okay to cheat on someone, regardless of what that person (or another person) has done to you in the past.

♦ Whatever you don't feed will die.

♦ No weapon formed against you shall prosper.

Chapter 5

BLESSING IN THE STORM

True friendships stand the test of time; destructive relationships don't. As I mentioned, eventually things died down with Dean, and I ended up breaking things off with him completely. This was easy, considering I'd redirected all of my energy and attention back to Mike. By now, I was under the assumption that we were always meant to be together. He would leave love songs playing in my car that would greet me on the morning ride to work. We attended events together, and I brought him around my friends, making it known that Dean was a thing of the past and that Mike and I were back on.

Just as before, things were very physical in terms of our relationship, often times frivolous and free. We made love in the nightclub, in the car, in the stairwell of my apartment building—whatever produced the most thrill. I was totally distracted and blinded by this relationship. I had not mentally healed from the drama in my past relationship, I had not addressed the concerns of our previous relationship, nor did I care about who he might have been seeing. To me, it was me and him. He made it clear that he was happy that I was back in his life, so I hung on to that idea for dear life, and didn't dare question the authenticity of his word, which was music to my ears.

Months later, while making a Target run with my daughter one Saturday afternoon, it dawned on me that I hadn't had a period in a while. I couldn't remember the last time I had purchased maxi pads. I grabbed a package of pads and slipped a pregnancy test deep down in my basket.

On the way home, I had a gut feeling that I was already pregnant. I could feel it the moment I had that revelation in Target. Actually, this wouldn't have been the first time I was pregnant by Mike; this would have been the third, since I'd had two abortions my first go-around with him.

The first one, I was scared out of my mind, didn't know what to expect, thought I was going to die right there on the table. Tears ran down my eyes as I was injected with the anesthesia. I woke up sobbing, and continued for hours and hours that day.

The second time, no tears. Read a magazine as I waited, counted down from ten while the anesthesia went in my arm, and woke up asking the nurse immediately for painkillers, to get a jumpstart on the pain. The second time I was numb to the fact that I was killing a life. Thoughts of that time really scared me.

My pregnancy test came back positive. I couldn't wait until Monday morning to call and make an appointment with my OB for confirmation. The entire time I was thinking, *Now what, Emily? What do you do?*

I started going through my mental Rolodex of examples of relationships that progressed to marriage after the birth of a child. I could've actually named at least three off the top of my head. *This could work,* I thought. *It could.*

Then doubt crept in. I needed some advice.

I met up with my girlfriends that night and asked them "hypothetically," what they thought of Mike and I having a baby.

"Hell to the no!" one of them responded. "I can't see it. Why would you even think about having a child by someone who has cheated on you in the past? Why put yourself through that?"

They didn't stop there. They went on and on and on, bringing up our love triangle, and my most recent drama with Dean.

"Thank God you didn't have a baby by that psychopath!"

One friend closed with this: "I know you are having fun. Mike *is* fun. But that's about it. Eventually you will find a real boyfriend and dump him soon anyway."

The next morning my dad met me over at my apartment. It was that time of the month when he came to visit me at my church. We gathered at the Forum in Inglewood, and to my surprise we had a guest speaker.

I thought to myself, *I really hope he's good. I could definitely use a word from the Lord today.* And, boy, did I receive one. I don't remember the preacher's name that day, but I sure remembered his message.

He asked, "Who in this audience is pregnant with God's blessing and afraid to give birth because of what other people are going to say? Huh? Who's willing to trust God and allow Him to bring out His will in your life, by giving birth to what He has planted in your life?"

I think I stood up out of my seat, raised my hand, and said, "Me, Lord, me!" I didn't think twice, at least not while in church service. It was one of those moments when I knew God was talking to me, through the preacher.

On the way home, I asked my dad, "When can you be clear

God is telling you to do something?"

He went on to say, "You know, sometimes we have a subtle feeling about something. Deep down, that could be God. Or while we are reading the Bible, He can speak to us. And sometimes He speaks through our minister or whoever is delivering the Word. That was a good sermon today, wasn't it, babe? I received that one."

"I received it, too."

I was able to get a same-day appointment the next day on Monday, and sure enough, my blood work came back positive. I thought to myself, *Lord, I am having another baby.*

As soon as I finished that thought, I thought of someone totally unexpected: Devin. It had been a while since we had talked. I hadn't filled him in on my latest relationship drama. All I wanted to tell him was that I had my very first "God moment." It was evident that God had spoken to me, and I couldn't think of anyone else to share this good news with but him. You see, the last time we spoke Devin had told me about all of the strides he had taken to get closer to God, attending church more frequently and joining different ministries. He also told me to get a study Bible and to try to read it often. I must admit, I had been so busy dealing with my breakup with Dean, and now fooling around with Mike, I hadn't even taken the plastic off the new Bible he'd recommended. Nonetheless, I gave him a call, wanting to share the good news. When I got no answer, I left a voice mail.

Meanwhile, Mike was on his way over. I had texted him to say I had something very important to tell him. Once he arrived, I told him immediately what had happened at church, and what the preacher had said, and that I felt that I needed to be obedient.

His first words were, "Wait, I may be missing something.

Are you trying to tell me that you're pregnant?"

I had been rambling so much about my God moment, I must have left out that small detail. "Yes, Mike, I am pregnant, and God told me to have this baby."

He paused for a long time and, with a blank stare on his face, said, "Okay."

I'm looking at him like, *Hello, that's it? Just okay?*

He repeated it again, this time with a little more firmness, "Okay." He told me he had to run and would be back to see me tomorrow, gave me a hug, and a small peck, and repeated it again, "Okay."

As I closed the door behind him, my phone began to ring. It was Devin calling me back. I hurried to answer the phone before I missed his call.

He said, "It's funny that I had a missed call from you. In fact, I was going to call you today anyway."

"Oh, that's funny. What were you going to call me about?"

"I've been thinking a lot lately about the past, about our friendship, and basically was wondering what you thought about us giving it another shot."

Clearly, I had heard him wrong, so I asked for him to repeat himself.

"What do you think about us getting back together, silly?"

His timing couldn't have been any worse. Flattered as I may have been, I just had to tell him the reason why I was calling him that day. I told him about my God moment and my decision to have the baby.

"By Mike or by the crazy dude?"

"By Mike."

Dead silence.

"Hello, are you still there? Hey, what's wrong?"

Then he answered ever so sadly, "You are starting your family without me."

My heart dropped. Right then I was so confused by my swirling emotions. *What have I done? What am I doing?*

Devin went ahead and ended the call with a generic, "Take care of yourself, and good luck with your baby."

I hung up the phone thinking, *Wow! If there was ever a chance of Devin and I rekindling anything, that chance is now gone.*

I didn't dwell on that for too long. I was having a baby by another. Clearly, I couldn't stay in that place. Besides, things had changed quickly between Mike and me after that.

A month or so went by, and it was now time to tell Emani the big news. I had a great idea to announce the pregnancy to both his daughter and mine at the same time. I was sure they would be delighted. But Mike thought it would be better if he told her himself, which was fine with me.

Mike came by for the announcement. I told Emani that she was going to have a little brother or sister, and she immediately squealed, "Yaaaayyyy! Mommy, you are pregnant!" Then she looked at Mike, ran to him squealing, and said, "Now you can be my Daddyyyyy!"

As Emani ran toward him to jump in his arms, he placed

his arms down and outward to block her embrace.

I thought to myself, *Did he just block my baby?*

Emani noticed it too and just stood there by him, downcast a bit, and then reclaimed her joy, turned around and hugged me instead. I couldn't help but think how strange a reaction that was. Why did he not want to embrace her? Why did he reject her?

After that incident, Mike became more and more distant. I was so taken aback by his actions. Why was he reverting to his old ways of being a mystery, of being MIA?

One evening we were driving home from dinner, and I simply asked him, "Why are you acting so strange since the pregnancy? You haven't come with any plans to get married or move in together. What's going on with you?"

He stuttered, "I-I-I'm still seeing someone."

My heart started pounding, and my palms grew sweaty. "You are seeing someone, huh?"

He nodded.

"Is this someone, Lauren?"

"Yes, yes, it's her."

I immediately went off. "Well, guess what? You need to stop seeing her, because we're getting ready to have a baby, gotdammit! Who has time to play these silly games with you? I don't. We don't. We are bringing another child into this world. Does that mean anything to you? Call it off, and call it off now, so we can move on with our lives."

"Okay, okay, I'll do it. I'm sorry. It'll be over, I promise."

♦

It was ultrasound day, time to find out the sex. I just knew it was a boy, a son of my very own. Between the two of us, we already had two girls, so a boy would've just made our family complete.

"What? It's a girl? Please, no. Can you check again?"

Mike just stood there laughing, but I didn't think it was funny.

After he dropped me off at the house, he said to me, "Wow! You are really sad about this. Are you going to cry?"

"Maybe."

"Why?"

"Mike, I really wanted a boy for *you*, someone who would be your sidekick, someone to carry on your name, you know, your MJ."

MJ was the name he would often tease me with during times I thought I was pregnant but was just late on my period. All jokes when you aren't really pregnant. But, yeah, he used to ask, "Is little MJ in there? Are you in there, buddy?"

Well, there would be no MJ coming from here. More like a Michaela or Mikea. I was pissed. I went on like this for several days. Every time someone asked, "What are you having?" I would say, "Another girl," and kept right on walking.

One evening on my way home from work, I got a call from a number that looked familiar. I answered, and it was Lauren. I let out the biggest sigh ever. "Yes, how may I help you?"

"I notice that you and Mike have started back talking."

I reminded her, "It's been some time since we rekindled things." Reflecting on my last instructions to Mike to call it off with her a few weeks prior, I asked her, "Are you two still seeing each other?"

Lauren cleared her throat. "Yeah, we're still together."

To say the least, I was disgusted with the way the conversation was going. I was thinking, *Do I tell her I am pregnant, or should I wait for Mike to tell her?*

I had hardly completed my thought, when she said, "Well, I was just calling to tell you that I am pregnant … with Mike's son. I'm due any day now."

I pulled over immediately because I started feeling lightheaded and dizzy. I asked her the due date, and sure enough it was only days away.

"Well, guess what, honey? I'm pregnant, too, with his daughter. Her name is Kennedy. I am five months, due in August."

She'd called me with that nonsense, only to get some breaking news in return. I had one second of "retaliation excitement" before the anger seeped in. *You mean to tell me that Mike had this girl pregnant the entire time I was pregnant? He knew the day I came to him with my God moment and he didn't say a word? He kept this from me my entire pregnancy? How could I have not known this?*

I called Mike and tore him a new one. I hated him. I demanded answers. I needed to know why he didn't say anything and why he allowed me to do this.

"You know firsthand what I experience with Emani's dad being absent; why would you do this to me again? Why, Mike? Why?"

He agreed to come by later that night and explain things.

I was on my way to have my hair done, and as you can imagine, I don't remember any details about that appointment. I sat in the chair for over two hours just running through my crazy life in my head.

I knew Mike had started acting strange immediately after our decision to have the baby. As I thought it through, it dawned on me that I hadn't seen Monica, his daughter in a while, probably before I had started showing. I recall him insisting that he would tell her himself, but I hadn't seen her since. Knowing him, I was sure she didn't even know. I hadn't been by his aunt's house where he lived, and I hadn't seen any of his cousins, coworkers, or friends.

Anger quickly turned into sadness and shame. I was still "the other woman," still a secret. Now my unborn daughter was "the other child."

Oh, Emily, how could you have let this happen? Lord, You told me to have this baby. This can't be you letting things happen this way. I feel like I am being punished by You, God. Lord, why do You hate me so much?

Mike came by later that night. I was broken, and he could see every piece of me shattered as soon as he walked in the door, since I had been sobbing for the past few hours. That might have been the first time he had ever seen me cry.

"Emily, I am sorry. Please forgive me. Let me explain."

"What can you possibly have to say?"

"The day you'd told me you were pregnant, and that you'd heard from God that you were meant to have the baby, I didn't want to say anything to prevent you from carrying out God's plan."

"Oh, so now you are all religious on me? Great!"

"See, if I had told you she was pregnant, you wouldn't have gone through with the pregnancy."

He was right on with that one. If I knew, I would have chosen to go my own way, politely asked God for His forgiveness, and made the first appointment available for an abortion. And I would have wished Mike and his new family a happy ever-after. I had been there before with these two. There was no way I was going to compete with them any longer, especially not with a child.

To this day, I know deep in my heart that my daughter Kennedy was a Godsend, protected and covered by unfortunate circumstances to ensure her very existence. No doubt, she was a by-product of the very first time I'd heard God's voice loud and clear, with specific instructions, that I actually obeyed. God used her father Mike to make sure that plan was executed, by keeping him silent. God sure does work in mysterious ways.

♦

For the next four months, I prayed to God to take my baby. I literally prayed for a miscarriage day and night. I didn't want to execute God's plan; I didn't want to carry this cross. I didn't want a daughter born into this love triangle that I hated so much.

This was clearly a moment where I not only thanked God, but shouted and danced that he did not answer my prayers. My daughter is awesome, a true blessing from the heavens. However, being totally transparent, I didn't always feel this way.

The relationship with Mike changed drastically. I was so distracted by what was happening that trying to make amends with him was the farthest thing from my mind. I literally wished I could never speak to him again then quickly thought, *That's what she wants—Mike all to herself and her baby.* I wasn't about to give her that satisfaction.

I was depressed no doubt but managed to push through. There were a few moments where time seemed to just stop, and then life kept on going. The first moment was when Lauren had her baby, about a week or so after her phone call.

I noticed Mike hadn't been calling to check on me. So I called him instead. No answer. A day or so passed, and he finally returned my call.

"She had her baby, didn't she?"

He said, "Yes, she did, and we almost lost him."

Although I muttered a "thank you God, your son is OK", just hearing him use the term *we* made my heart stop beating. The thoughts of me carrying and raising this child alone while he was with her and their son was just indescribable.

Another time, Monica, his daughter, came by the house for the first time in a long time. It seemed like her warm, bubbly persona had changed just seeing me pregnant. She was now seven going on eight, and had grown much taller since I last saw her. This time, I was not greeted with a hug, nor a smile. My excitement to see her soon met her non-excitement to see me.

"So you are having a girl, huh?"

"Yes, you'll have a little sister."

"Well, I hope she's not born on my birthday."

My due date was a day after her birthday. "Okay, I'll see what I can do, but I won't make any promises." Monica never once mentioned that her brother was born. Nor did she mention Lauren.

It seemed like she was now in a world full of secrets, a world her father created, and which she had now grown accustomed to and found her place in.

♦

Fast-forward a few months, and it was almost game time for me. Mike's family showed up at my baby shower more as a show of support than to welcome my new baby, or so it seemed. I received long hugs, fake smiles, and "everything-is-going-to-be-all-right" pats on my back. Several of his friends also came, although without their wives or significant others, so it was clear to me where their allegiance lay—with her, of course.

Mike and I wore coordinated outfits and put on a show that we were a lovely couple expecting a beautiful baby girl. He helped me pack up my truck with all the gifts and then rushed off, once the car was unloaded. He always seemed to be in a hurry these days. I internalized it as, *He's off to be with his real family.*

A few weeks later, on my last day of work before I went on maternity leave, I was at my sister's house celebrating with a fantastic meal she had prepared for me, while she and my best friend Stacy drank wine.

Mike called, sounding all perky. "Just checking on you," he said. "I haven't heard from you in a few days. Everything okay with my little princess in there?"

"Everything's fine. I'm having dinner, and I plan to go for a walk later."

"Do you need me to come over?"

Hell no, I thought, but I politely told him, "No, that's okay. I'm doing fine." I hung up the phone thinking, *Hmm, that was odd.*

It was three am the next morning when I started having labor pains at my apartment. I called Mike but got no answer. Then I called my sister as a backup, and she came right over. I was in full labor, with contractions kicking in and dilating a lot faster than my previous pregnancy.

Everyone was calling Mike, but there was still no answer. I started to worry. *Will he miss my delivery? Is this how Kennedy's life is starting? Without her father nearby?*

My teenage niece decided to send him a chirp through my Nextel phone. "Mike! If you can hear me, Emily is in labor. You need to get here and get here fast."

Sure enough, I received a call soon after from him. "I'm on my way. Wait for me."

"You need to hurry up." Deep down in my core, I knew he had to have been over Lauren's house.

Mike happened to be there for me during the hardest part of my delivery, one hand in mine, the other holding a video camera. "Baby girl, your mommy is a gangster, and you'll grow up to be just as strong, smart and beautiful as she is".

He was right, Kennedy *was* beautiful. She cried a lot, but she was beautiful.

The next day in the hospital, I was desperately trying to soothe Kennedy.

Mike came over from the couch, picked her up, laid her on his chest, and she was quiet immediately.

I thought, *What the heck! She loves him already. Little does she know, her father is an* A-*hole.* Then it dawned on me. *This little girl doesn't care. Already she knows that is her daddy, and she loves him, no matter what.*

Right there and then, I made a promise to her and to myself to never discredit Mike's name or character, and to allow her to decide on her own what type of father and man he is, and for them to establish their own relationship. And I've kept that promise.

It took several years to get over the hurt and pain Mike caused, and a lot of effort to not take my circumstances out on this innocent child, who clearly did not ask to be here. I surpassed depression, jealousy, envy, and hopelessness. I must admit, God is a good God.

I have to give it to Mike. Over the years, he made sure that MJ and Kennedy spent as much time as possible; they were best of friends by the time they were three and have been ever since. Their bond and love for each other is no one but God.

Lauren and I grew to be cordial, and once she moved on from Mike herself, things even got better between us. We both are happily married, talk often, and our kids see each other, outside of their scheduled visits with their dad. We aren't BFFs like we once said we would be back in the day when we'd first found out about each other and started hanging out. Too much had happened for a true friendship to exist. But we do manage to sustain a relationship beyond cordial, for the sake of our children.

Lessons Learned

♦ Listen to God, and do not assume that the journey after your decision will be peaches and cream.

♦ Through every trial, you will come THROUGH.

♦ God will not bless your mess, but He can leave you with a blessing.

♦ Having baby momma/baby daddy drama is a decision. You can decide to keep up the drama, or you can decide to swallow your pride, leave the past behind you, and be the better person and make your situation the best situation for your children.

♦ You don't have to be BFFs, but be cordial with your ex's baby mommas, ex-wife, etc. This is for the sake of the children, who didn't ask to be here.

♦ Control negative self-talk. What you think about and harp on, you will attract in you. If you dwell on drama, you'll attract drama. If you think about moving on and the endless possibilities that lie ahead, you will attract opportunity and new beginnings.

Chapter 6

FLAWS AND ALL

For years, I thought that no one would want me, not with two kids by two different fathers, and that marriage, or even dating, was out of the question for me. I was prepared to be lonely, to die alone.

I took a short break on dating or even trying to meet guys, all stemming from my negative thinking. I wasn't sure how to explain my two out-of-wedlock children, so I avoided having the conversation altogether by not talking to men, period.

That worked for a while, until a fine piece of caramel by the name of Sebastian walked into my office. He had come for an interview as a transfer from another department. Considering he was coming to see my boss and I was filling in for her assistant at the time, I just had to speak to him, right? This interaction was permissible, so I took full advantage.

"Coffee or tea while you wait?" I couldn't take my eyes off him, but something was slightly off, though. *Why is someone this tall and handsome holding his head down?*

My eyes stayed fixed on him until he finally raised his head up and looked me in the eye. Why in the heck did he do that? I could have melted when his beautiful green eyes met mine. Then he topped off the whole interaction with one of the best smiles I had ever seen. I'm talking Michael Ealy with added height. God had peeked down from the heavens just to give me a little caramel treat for the day. I still liked men; I loved them actually. That was all the reassurance I needed.

Of course, I received five emails from five different coworkers wanting to know who in the hell was that. Women were going on their third and fourth break just to walk past my boss's glass door. I thought it was pretty funny that one good-looking guy could cause so much commotion in a department.

Well, my boss must have been just as mesmerized as we were because, within a week, Sebastian was hired. Damn it! Now I had to look at him every day. Good thing his cubicle was way down the hall.

It didn't take long for the rumors to start circulating about him—Sebastian has a girlfriend who lives in New York; he has a son; he doesn't date black women, and on and on. I didn't feel the need to get to know him for myself. I just thought of him as some hot guy who now worked in our department. I must say though, he was polite and spoke quite often.

One afternoon I walked down the hall and asked one of my close girlfriends if she wanted to go grab something to eat.

Sebastian, who happened to be around, turned around in his chair and politely said, "I'm hungry. Can I join you ladies?"

"Uuuummmm, okay," I said, figuring it wouldn't be any harm. Then I turned into the conversationalist that I am, asked about his son, if he was dating, basically trying to confirm if there was any substance to any of the rumors flying around.

He did confirm he was dating someone who lived in New York. He also made it a point to mention that she was of Indian descent. I liked the fact that he was so open with me and didn't seem to hide or sugarcoat anything in terms of his long-distance relationship.

Talking about her in high regard was admirable to say the least. I told him that I thought that was awesome, she sounded great actually, and that I wished him the best in their relationship.

He kind of shrugged his shoulders like, *Eh, we'll see.*

That shrug of the shoulders, inconsistent with the spiel I'd just heard, threw me off a bit.

Several weeks later I was sitting at cheerleading practice with another coworker-turned-good friend, Camille. We were chit-chatting about work, life, how things were going with Mike.

I shook my head from side to side. "Girl, we are so done."

She then asked, "Well, do you feel you are ready to start dating again?"

I paused for a second and thought. "Sure, I would be down."

She didn't hesitate before responding, "Good! Because I have something to tell you."

"What, girl? What do you have to tell me?"

"Well, I was at lunch with Sebastian the other day, and out of nowhere, he asked, 'What's the deal with Emily?' So, of course, I talked you up—I told him you were super smart, educated, and a great mom."

"Did he ask about my kids' father?"

"Well, yes. Naturally, he asked if you were married before and if the kids were by the same dad."

My heart started racing. "So, what did you say?"

"I told him I wasn't sure."

I breathed a sigh of relief. A feeling of sadness overran me, realizing that my friend felt the need to lie about my situation.

Camille smiled. "I think he likes you."

"Wait a minute. What the hell, Camille? I thought he was with "New York". "New York" was the office nickname for Sebastian's girlfriend, since no one seemed to know her name.

"Well, things don't seem to be going so well with those two, from the looks of things."

Wow! I thought.

Well, needless to say, my friend Camille, aka matchmaker, must have gone back with her bow and arrow, trying to make a love connection, because I got an email from him the very next day.

We chatted for a while, and sure enough he asked me out to lunch one afternoon. So we went, and long story short, I'd had better first dates. But it was memorable enough. I learned about what was going on with his now ex-girlfriend, more about his son, what he liked to do.

My first impression was, he was a bit uppity. I couldn't wait to ask his dating preferences.

"I date all women," he said, "no real preference."

Yeah, yeah. That's what all guys who date outside of their race tell an African American woman.

Later back in the office, I received another email from him, asking me out on another date, outside of office hours this time. A real date. I wasn't expecting it, but I went for it anyway. We scheduled our date for later in the week, and I volunteered to pick him up from his friend's house.

When I picked him up, I realized I was overdressed. I wore my typical date-night attire—cute jeans, dressy flowing top, and high heels—while he had on a T-shirt, jeans, and Chucks. I remember thinking, *Wow! You are really embarrassing yourself with this one, Em.*

Soon my focus was off me and on him, with his Tupac T-shirt on.

"What the heck do you know about Tupac?"

And I went on to explain how I thought he was a little whitewashed, and would have never guessed he listened to rap music. He got a good laugh out of that one.

As we were on our way to dinner, listening to music, I saw him grooving in my passenger seat, with slow, sensuous moves.

I laughed nervously. I think I was getting a bit turned on. Remember, it had been a while. *Pull it together, Em* was all I kept saying to myself. *Pull it together.*

We had an enjoyable evening. I took him back to his friend's house and was awaiting that awkward moment. The first kiss. I knew it was going to happen; I could tell by the overall chemistry of the night.

Well, the first kiss was whack, simply put. He knew it and

I knew it. However, on his suggestion, we tried it again. Nailed it.

A few more lunch dates went by, evening talks on the phone, and he finally encouraged me to talk about the situation with Mike, which I had avoided for several weeks.

He demanded to know what happened in my last relationship, specifically with my daughter's father. I finally told him that my girls had different dads, and about the drama I went through with Mike and Lauren.

Fifteen minutes into my rant, he cut me off. "You aren't over him."

"What! Of course, I'm over him."

"No, you aren't. You are still in love with this guy."

"No, sir, you are wrong, I get nauseous when I think about the situation; still in love is a bit exaggerated."

"Okay, well, if you aren't in love, you definitely haven't healed from it all."

In hindsight, he was dead on.

As time went on, we continued with our lunch dates, or I would visit Sebastian at his friend's house, have a drink, and spend the evening listening to music, make out, and go home. This went on for about a month.

I realized things were getting more serious the night that I met his brother and his brother's girlfriend, whom he talked so kindly of. When I first met the two, I wasn't surprised to see that his brother's girlfriend wasn't black. She wasn't even mixed. She was a fair-skinned Latina with long, wavy hair. But there was nothing awkward about this chick at all because she was cool as heck.

I did notice that she followed her man's eyes when he was introduced to me. She had that "I wonder if he finds this black girl attractive" type of look. Me, I was just taking it all in.

We rode with them to a nightclub where his friend was performing that night. Her brand-new Mercedes truck put my five-year-old Mercedes to shame.

Once we got there, the four of us all immediately went to the bar and started on some shots and margaritas. Before you know it, Ms. Latina and I were drunk BFFs for the night, and the brothers were having a great time grooving to the music.

I asked her, "Do you think you guys will get married?"

"Heck, yeah! I just know we are!"

Yelling over the music, I asked his brother, "Do you think she's the one?"

"I know she's the one."

I smiled with the biggest grin. I saw that type of love in them and wanted it immediately.

"My brother is really digging you, by the way. He can't stop talking about you."

"Really?" That was all I really needed to hear.

Between the Patrón and the slightest confirmation that Sebastian liked me, the fix was in.

It had to have been, because I had no recollection of what happened after I dropped my purse at the bar and all of my belongings spilled out on the floor.

Watching him pick up every single last item off the floor, I squealed, "Awweee, he really does like me! Look at him pick up my things!"

Yeah, silly me. That's all I needed to go back home with him obviously, because I woke up the next morning completely naked, hungover, and lying right beside my hot coworker turned lunch buddy turned booty call.

The guilt immediately sank in. "Oh my God, I can't believe I am here with you." Tears ran down my face. "I am a hoe-mom! How did I let this happen?"

Sebastian jumped up. "No, no. You aren't a hoe-mom. Last night was beautiful."

He gently grabbed the back of my neck, and I jerked away. My head hurt, I felt like crap, and I probably looked like crap. I just wasn't ready.

"How about that shower, though?"

"Shower?"

"Wow! You *really* don't remember anything?"

"Absolutely not."

He did a recap of the previous night's events. From the shower to the full body massage, he went on and on about how our first sexual encountered played out.

That following morning when I went home, I was hesitant to turn the key to my apartment. My mother had come over to watch the girls for me that evening and definitely didn't expect me to stay out all night.

She just looked at me with a smirk. "Hope you had fun," she said.

♦

I went to work that Monday morning with my head hanging pretty low, not sure what to expect, wondering if he would tell my girlfriend about what happened. And, of course, he did.

I asked her, "Well, what did he say?"

"Oh, he just said that you guys went to the concert, oh, and had sex later that night."

"Oh, just great!"

After I asked for more details, she said, "His exact words were, 'Much better than I expected, even though she didn't remember anything.'"

Right then, I thought it would be over. Yet again, he kept on pursuing things until eventually we became a couple. Whether or not I was ready for another relationship was probably still up in the air. I knew this time, I took a totally different approach. I had experienced the finer things in the dating world and realized it wasn't all it was cracked up to be at all. This guy was different, surrounded by a totally different culture than what I was used to, so I had to set myself apart somehow, by studying the women surrounding him.

You see, Sebastian had a very strong group of core friends. I would say about five, six if you included his brother, all black men either married to or dating non-black women. Well, some were actually biracial. And the black girl, didn't even consider herself fully black. She was half Puerto Rican, or black Spanish as she called herself. I was the only one who considered herself black.

I found out some very interesting things about this group. They all smoked weed, which I thought was funny. Here we were in west LA with all these bougie, mixed or non-black girls sitting around in a circle and smoking. They still had the same concerns as black girls, they still talked trash, they still argued, and they still didn't take any crap from their men. And there was also talk about infidelity, the same ole, same ole that we black girls experience.

Now I did notice that these girls made some money. In fact, most of them made six figures. Yes, I was slightly behind at that time, but I chalked it up to the age difference. And they all lived in neighborhoods I wasn't used to, like Pasadena and West LA, and owned nice homes. They were all very generous with their men, paying for meals, buying plane tickets and sponsoring trips, and fixing up rooms in their apartments exclusively for their boyfriend's kids.

One couple had to move out of their apartment abruptly and didn't have a place to live. Had that happened to me, I would have been on my sister's couch. But this couple was able to stay with a friend in Beverly Hills in their guest home (not room, but home) for a few months until they found a house of their own. In another instance, this girl who worked for a prominent philanthropist was gifted $400K to purchase her first home. Who knows of anyone who would give anybody $400K toward their first home? Crazy. It didn't surprise me one bit that these black men were holding on pretty tight to these women, despite the usual arguments or troubles they might have had. They had it too good.

Considering I wanted to prove myself in our relationship, I adopted some of these same habits. I would treat more often than I was treated, I would buy him clothes, I would slip money into his pockets whenever I heard he was low. Sebastian had an entry level position at my company, and was an aspiring photographer, so I invested in his first professional grade camera. It cost me about a thousand dollars, but hey, I was investing in his future.

I can't go on without saying he had a great family, a sister who was just phenomenal, and mother, aunt, and nephews all sweet as can be. They welcomed the girls and I with open arms. I had never experienced such a sense of community, of being a part of a large family as well as a large circle of friends. I loved being included. Being one of the girls in the friend crew was what I always yearned for with Mike, and finally I had that with Sebastian.

All of these things covered up major red flags that I saw early on in our relationship. Yes, he was gorgeous; I knew that from jump. But I didn't like that he flirted with almost everything alive. I caught him flirting with coworkers, young and old, his homeboys' girlfriends, and even his sister-in-law; he didn't discriminate. He also drank quite often, but I couldn't say too much about that because I was usually going in right along with him.

Other times, he just missed the mark. He once threw me a surprise birthday party, at a beautiful restaurant, in the hills with the most gorgeous view of LA. It was about fifteen of us. Only four guests were friends of mine—my sister and her boyfriend, and Camille and her boyfriend. I kept looking at the door, hoping for more of *my* friends to show up, considering it was a surprise party for me. Well, come to find out, they weren't invited.

He later explained that he didn't feel that his friends and my friends would mix well. In that case, I thought, all of my friends should have been invited and his friends should've stayed home.

One time he purchased a new car, a two-seater Nissan. I asked him, "Why did you buy a two-seater?"

His response was, "One seat for me, one seat for Aaron (his son)."

"Oookaaayyy. What if my car broke down, or you had to pick up my kids? We couldn't even fit in the car. Did you ever think of that?" My point fell on deaf ears.

For whatever reason, he didn't let me get too close to Aaron. He was about a year older than Emani, and those two got along great. Kennedy actually took to him quite well too. I always wanted a boy and thought it would be a perfect opportunity to get close to his son. Perhaps he thought differently.

Another time, I had just received a huge promotion on the job. Everyone was congratulating me, sending me emails left and right, giving me high-fives throughout the hallway, handshakes from superiors, and plenty of "well deserved, Emily"s. All from everyone except Sebastian. When I finally reached out to him, asking had he heard the news, his response was "Yes, I heard. Funny that you got the job, guess they needed that token Black girl after all". *Really, token Black girl? How 'bout congratulations babe, you deserve it?* Although his response hurt, I chose not to bring it up. I knew he wasn't happy with where he was in his career. Besides, I wanted to marry this man, flirtatious ways and all. I loved his friends, his family, and wanted it all, ignoring the deep-seeded feeling that surfaced periodically.

We were once at a dance show for my daughter, and as he looked up on stage and saw this little mixed girl with long, big, bushy curly hair dancing around, he said, "Awww, I want a daughter."

I thought, *What the hell! You already have two potential daughters. They just don't look like her.*

All this, and things just got even worse.

I didn't trust him. I hated when he drank too much. We would argue quite a bit.

He broke up with me quite often, saying, "I don't need this

crap. I'm out of here," only to come running back a few days later with an apology.

Of course, I would give in, but just the thought of it being that easy for him to say didn't sit well with me at all.

I started going to counseling, wondering why I was encountering some of the same problems as in previous relationships. I couldn't trust this man. Even though I didn't have any hard evidence, there was something in the pit of my stomach that told me that there was someone else. I was becoming jealous of his relationship with his sister, his sister-in-law, and his female friends.

Due to my insecurities, I started my internal investigation. I wanted to know who he was talking to, whether or not he was cheating on me, and with whom. I was looking through phone records, voice mails, emails, the whole nine, for evidence of cheating. I did find out that he talked quite often to one friend more than I was comfortable with. He also left me a few times to go have drinks with a female married coworker, who was, you guessed it, non-black. That caused a huge argument.

Despite us breaking up over that incident, I continued my investigation and found a voice mail on his work phone from an older woman, it seemed, who wished him luck on an upcoming photoshoot that he had with his brother and sister-in-law.

I listened to the message thinking, *How the heck did she know about that shoot?* They had to have talked often. What took the cake were the words "I love you" at the end of the voice mail, all sweet and endearing. I was pissed. I finally found the evidence I was searching for. And it felt just like before, only worse. All of the advice I got from his sister, the girlfriends, his mom, all on how to be a better mate to him, none of it worked.

Out of rage, I wanted everyone to know that he was full of

it, that he had put on this facade of being this great guy and I was the crazy one. Well, it was time to show them crazy. I started typing, and typing, and typing and couldn't stop. I can't quite recall all that I wrote, but I typed a very long, detailed email, and blind-copied every single person I knew was connected to him. Family, friends, people who were on group emails, whoever knew him, and I had record of their email were on the BCC line.

I thought twice about sending it. Actually, I had my new coworker read it. She tended to be a "Bitter Betty" at times, and I just knew she would be all for it.

To my surprise, her response was, "Oh shit! Em, do not send that email. Do not send it."

"I want them to know he hurt me. If I press this send button, I could never go back to him or show my face again, so I know this would be final this time." By now we were on breakup number three.

Bitter Betty said, "I wouldn't do that if I were you."

I called my sister, Aretha and told her what happened. She said, "You know what? If I were you, I would send that damn email."

That's all I needed to hear. I just needed one confirmation. I pressed send.

About ten minutes later, I got the longest email I have ever received in my life. It was from his sister, tearing me a new one. I read the whole thing three times. One thing that stood out was her perceived point of my email: to discredit her brother.

Hmmm, she was right. Obviously, discrediting him didn't work for her; it did the exact opposite. She could have never loved her little brother more than that day, after his psycho ex-girlfriend tried to run his name in the mud.

After reading her email, I felt worse than the piece of gum stuck under my cubicle desk.

Just then another email came in, from his mom. It read: EMILY, YOU SHOULD HAVE NEVER AIRED YOUR DIRTY LAUNDRY LIKE THIS. THIS CONVERSATION SHOULD HAVE BEEN BETWEEN YOU AND MY SON. I WISH YOU AND THE GIRLS THE BEST OF LUCK. PLEASE DON'T EVER EMAIL ME AGAIN.

By this time, I felt like the scum of the earth.

Another email came in, this time from his brother. His brother never emailed and hardly ever talked. He just smiled and nodded and was the nicest guy I had met in years. His email started off: ARE YOU FUCKING KIDDING ME, EMILY?

I didn't read the rest of it. I couldn't take any more.

I forwarded my original email to my therapist. Clearly, we had some things to talk about later. I also created a rule in my outlook messages deleting all related messages. I named that rule "Hate mail."

Only one email came through, and it had no subject line. It was from the wife of one of his friends. It read: I AM SORRY FOR YOUR PAIN, AND I PRAY THAT YOU ARE HEALED.

I finally broke down after that and left my office that day in a daze.

On the drive home my therapist called and said, "Why did you write that?"

Sobbing, I said, "I don't know. Do you think I am crazy?"

She said, "No, you aren't crazy, you were just mad. Let's get you in ASAP."

As you might've guessed, that was the end of that relationship. I hated myself for that incident and didn't talk much about it afterwards. I told a few friends about what I had done, but it was definitely nothing that I bragged about. If I am not mistaken, I did send out a formal apology but didn't get a response from many people. Or maybe I'd created a rule to delete those too; I don't quite remember.

It was funny how any indiscretions that took place with Sebastian were totally drowned by my outrageous rage of revenge. Guess who looked like the fool at the end of the day? You guessed it—yours truly.

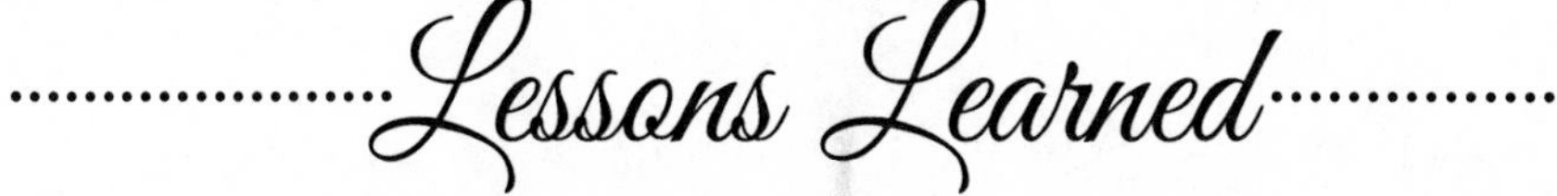

Lessons Learned

♦ Follow your gut. Pay attention to flirting; flirtatious ways may cause problems in the future.

♦ Watch out for comparing yourselves to other women, adapting their actions, in efforts to reap the same rewards you think they are receiving. Be yourself, to ensure you attract the right mate for you.

♦ Be cautious of very attractive men. It takes a very strong, self-confident woman to date an extremely good-looking man. Just like you're attracted to them, so are 90% of the other women in the room.

♦ Pay attention to the people who don't clap when you win, especially your significant other. That's a sure sign that perhaps they cannot take your success and all that your fabulous self brings.

♦ Regardless of how close you are to them, a man's family and friends will always hold an allegiance to him, not you. After you are long gone, he is still their boy, their brother, their son, and you are just a memory.

♦ Learn to control your crazy! Yes, you may get hurt; that's all a part of the dating game. But seeking revenge gets you nowhere. You end up embarrassed beyond measure, or in jail, looking like a fool instead of a victim. Hurt, heal, and move the hell on. God will take care of them.

HOW COME YOU DON'T CALL ME

After breaking up with Sebastian, I vowed to do things differently, to be more cautious about whom I was dating. At least that was the goal. The end of our relationship was still pretty new, so of course I sought comfort from my all-time best girlfriends in the entire world, my two big sisters Lynette and Aretha. They were the only ones who didn't think I was absolutely nuts after that email. They actually described my actions as brave and bold. Typical big sister behavior, finding the good in a hideous situation.

My consolation happened during a visit to San Antonio, where Lynette, my eldest sister lived. While she got her hair done that day by Miss Maddie, I was telling her all about what had happened.

You know that hair stylists are practically licensed psychologists, so Miss Maddie asked, "Well, what's your next plan?"

"On to the next," I said.

Before I could get even the words out of my mouth, my sister said, "Good! Because we have someone for you."

On cue, my eyes rolled in the back of my head. "Okay, who is it?"

Miss Maddie said, "Well, my son. Not asking too much of you guys, I just want him to meet you, that's it."

I thought to myself, *Well, hey, what the heck.* Now I really liked Miss Maddie. She was too cool, and she and my sister were good friends. Word on the street was, Miss Maddie had a football team of handsome sons, so I have to admit, I was curious to meet one of them myself.

He called later that afternoon, and I immediately thought, *These two work extremely fast.*

He asked if I wanted to go out and get a drink with him and his brothers, and I said, "Sure."

I tried to talk my twenty-one-year-old niece to come along, but the bar scene wasn't her deal. So I thought, *Hey, you only live once. I'll roll solo.*

When the doorbell rang, I really didn't know what to expect. I was anxiously waiting to see what all the hype was about. I opened the door and immediately thought, *Yep, they weren't lying. These dudes are fine.* I would describe them as country, corn-fed brothas, all three of them six three and upward, and stocky. Think football players leaving the locker room, all showered and leaving the stadium.

The one of interest to me, Jason, after introducing himself, laughed and joked with my brother-in-law. I got reacquainted with one brother, whom I had actually met the day before at a picnic my sister had. And the youngest brother, who was only about nineteen or twenty, but equally fine, stayed quiet. I just wondered how the night would go.

We all jumped into Jason's Hummer, and we talked on the way to the local bar. Once we got there, he opened the car door and door to the restaurant like a gentleman, asked if I wanted food, what I wanted to drink, the whole nine.

Cute and a gentleman? Jason was winning major points.

The other brothers were cool too, asking me about LA, and the ladies out there. We had a few beers and just shot the breeze. One brother told me about his baby momma issues, and the youngest one just said he was having fun, wasn't trying to settle down. But Jason really didn't talk much about his personal life, which I found interesting. On the way back home, I wanted to ask him so badly more questions about his relationship status, but we had an audience.

When we pulled up to my sister's house, he said politely, "Wow! That was more fun than I expected. Do you mind if we keep in touch?"

"Absolutely."

I turned toward the back seat to say goodbye to the middle brother, and as soon as our eyes connected, I saw him shaking his head vigorously from side to side. As in "no, don't do it!". By this time, Jason was on the other side of the car, opening my door. I played it off and said, "Well, nice meeting you."

♦

"How did it go?" Lynette asked, with brother-in-law and niece smiling in the background.

"It went okay; we plan to keep in touch."

My sister could have jumped for joy right in her living room. I didn't tell them about the strange gesture from the other brother, who I honestly thought was hating, and maybe wanted me for himself.

After my San Antonio trip, Jason and I did keep in touch. He texted me a few days later. In fact, he texted all the time: HOW ARE YOU? HOW WAS YOUR DAY? WHAT DID YOU DO THIS WEEKEND? ARE YOU WATCHING THE LAKERS GAME?

About two weeks after we started text-dating, I did finally get enough nerve to ask him his relationship status, and whether he was looking for a committed relationship, or having fun playing the field.

He responded: HAVING FUN PLAYING THE FIELD.

I can change that, I thought.

We texted each other back and forth for about a month. I'm sure I saw other guys from time to time, but Jason consumed most of my evenings and lunch breaks texting back and forth with him.

He started to say things like, IT'S SO EASY TO TALK TO YOU. YOU SEEM LIKE THE PERFECT GIRL. YOUR LAST GUY REALLY SCREWED UP.

Then the request for the pictures started rolling in. OH MY GOODNESS! YOU ARE SO BEAUTIFUL. SEND ME ANOTHER.

I would get a few too in return, which was cool.

Finally, I asked if we could talk on the phone, and we did. It was brief, but at least I got the chance to hear the man's voice.

Before his birthday came around, I was lucky enough to get another phone call. I casually said, "Well, for your birthday, how about coming to LA? I will host you, and your brothers could come."

"Nah, I think my friends have something planned for me. They aren't saying, so I'll have to take a rain check."

A little bummed, I said, "Okay."

Then I got with my sister, who happened to be a fantastic caterer in the area, to bake him a nice cake, and deliver it to his home. I also made him a nice card with a cute picture of myself on the front, and on the inside some sweet nothings about how I enjoyed our friendship, and happy birthday to a wonderful man, hope to see you soon. I sent the card overnight, to accompany my cake delivery for the next day, which was his actual birthday.

I spoke to him once via text earlier that day, wishing him happy birthday, but nothing since then, and it was now about four p.m. his time.

I called my sister. I asked her, "Did you deliver the cake?"

"Yeah, early this morning."

Hmmm.

The night went on and I didn't hear a thing. It seemed my little gesture of goodwill went unnoticed.

The following day (yes, the next day) he called me to thank me for my cake. He said, "Did you make that card?"

"Yes, I did."

"Nice."

I asked him what he did, and he said his friends surprised him with whitewater rafting or something like that. That was odd to me that he didn't know of that event, that it was a surprise.

Anyway, I guess I got over the whole birthday gesture fail and continued to text him. Eventually, I had had enough of the texting and decided to just be blunt with him.

"Look, we have been texting for a while, we talk on the phone ever so often, and I want to know if we have any true chemistry, if this friendship would ever lead to something. I want to see you. Fly me out there."

Surprisingly, he agreed. He agreed a little too fast for me. I didn't think that little rant was going to fly. Especially since it was something I'd initiated.

We set a date via text that was maybe two weeks away. I went ahead and purchased the ticket with the expectation that he would reimburse me.

Two days before my trip, I'm doing squats and sit-ups like crazy, and getting my outfits together. Then I got a call from him. I immediately answered.

He said, "I don't think this weekend will be good. My little brother needs money for summer school, and I'll be short on cash."

Typical me, I said, "That's okay. If it'll help, we can go half on the ticket."

He paused and said, "Nah, maybe we should do it another time."

"Look, it's just for the weekend. We don't have to do much. I just want us to spend real time together, see if we like each other. If not, we go our separate ways."

He finally agreed.

♦

I called Jason while exiting the plane to let him know I'd touched down. Then I got my bag from baggage claim, ran to the restroom to touch up my makeup. I checked myself in the mirror. I was feeling pretty good about myself, having lost five pounds for the trip. My hair was still cute, and I wore nice wedges, instead of tennis shoes, that really set off my hot-jet-setting-chic look I was going for.

I waited patiently at my phone for a text or phone call. No text. No phone call. Thirty minutes went by. I sat down and twiddled my thumbs. As you can guess, I was PISSED.

Jason finally arrived, and I met him at his truck. His clothes were wrinkled, his hair wasn't cut, and from the hug I had received, he smelled kind of stale.

I did all these darn squats, got a brand-new weave, new outfits, and this dude couldn't even shower or get a haircut.

We had lunch and went back to his apartment. I had planned for my sister, who lived about an hour away, to pick me up that evening. I'd wanted to set up some boundaries for the trip, so we'd agreed to absolutely no sex.

Well, I had about two hours to kill before my sister was scheduled to pick me up for the evening. A long two hours. The excitement of the months of text messaging and not seeing each other immediately kicked in. We got physical pretty quickly, with the kissing, heavy petting, and fondling. It felt good, a little too good.

I was so happy that phone rang. My sister called to tell me she was outside.

Jason walked me to the car with my small bag that I had packed for the night. He picked me up off the ground and gave me a big kiss right in front of my sister.

When I got in and he closed my door, and we got far enough away, both me and my sister screamed like teenagers. It was fun to see my conservative big sister so excited.

"You guys must be hitting it off pretty good so far," she said.

"Yeah, I guess so."

I failed to mention the part about him being late and not well groomed. Actually, I had forgotten all about that.

♦

The next morning, the deal was for me to ride back into Austin with my brother-in-law, and for Jason to pick me up from the firehouse where my brother-in-law worked. Again, this dude was a whole hour late picking me up the next morning.

My brother-in-law looked at me with that face. "Well, sis, maybe something came up."

When Jason got there, I had a little attitude by this time.

"What do you want to do?"

Of course, that didn't help either. *Does he not have a plan for us today?*

"Well, whatever you want to do is fine with me."

So he was quick on his toes, and he proceeded to show me around the city of Austin. He took me to an outdoor type of mall with high-end department stores that definitely piqued my interest. I liked it; I could see myself living there.

We then had lunch and then headed to a movie.

While we were trying to find a park, his phone rang. He didn't answer. The phone rang again, and again and again.

Finally, he answered, "What's up? … Nah, I didn't work today … I'm at the movies … Yeah, I'm alone … Hey, I will call you after, okay?"

Alone? Really, dude? I was stank the whole movie. I couldn't tell you to this day what movie we watched that afternoon.

That evening we headed to his house, and again he asked, "What should we do tonight?"

I was so irritated with this trip by now, I just told him, "Think of something."

We were watching a little TV while having a cocktail, when he got a call that he picked up on the first ring. Then after excusing himself, he came back and told me he got called in for overtime, that he thought he'd switched with a coworker but the schedule wasn't updated and they were expecting him.

So, yeah, the night we were supposed to be getting to know each other, I spent getting to know his little Wiener dog, Cindy. She was actually cool. I fed her, took a shower, and started a movie. She hopped on the bed, and I thought to myself, *Why not? Might as well keep me company.*

I fell asleep, but soon after I did hear him come in. I was so irritated about the whole ordeal, I faked sleep. Cindy slept between us that night. There was no kissing, no heavy petting, which was all right with me.

♦

The next morning, we got dressed, I got packed, and had breakfast before my flight. As he pulled up to the ATM, he asked, "How much do I owe you again for the flight?"

I told him, and he gave me his half only. *Ugh!*

Then we were off to the airport. He pulled up to the curb, gave me a nice hug, and was off.

After I checked in and went through security, I sat down and looked at my watch. I couldn't help but to bust up in laughter. I was forty-five minutes early for my flight. This fool couldn't wait to drop me off.

Considering I had so much time to kill waiting for my flight, I just replayed in my head what an epic failure the weekend was. Something just seemed off. I recalled an earlier conversation, during our initial texting days, when Jason had said he didn't have any social media accounts. I decided to plug in his name to Facebook to see if I found anything. Sure enough, a profile popped up, with his name and face, hugged up with some other chick, cheek to cheek.

I never confronted him about it. Our texting soon died down. It was obvious he wasn't *that* interested in me, nor was he even emotionally available. From what I heard from my sister, he continued to date the woman in his profile picture, until she was his fiancé and, eventually, until they were married. I was just thankful that things didn't get past heavy petting.

Lessons Learned

♦ The longer you are single, the more your friends and family will try to play matchmaker. Sure, try it, but if it doesn't feel right, don't be afraid to let them down easy. This is your life, your relationship, your future.

♦ If you want a committed relationship, and a guy tells you that he doesn't, that he's having fun playing the field, however he phrases it, believe him. Do not pass go, on to the next.

♦ If he only wants to text, there's a problem. Texting is not courting.

♦ If you have to initiate the phone calls, the dates, everything, all the time, he's just not that into you, and that's okay.

♦ Value a man that is on time, well groomed, and presentable when he picks you up for dates. It shows that he is putting forth effort in trying to impress you.

♦ If he cancels on you the first date, on to the next.

♦ If he lies to someone else, he will lie to you.

♦ If someone tries to warn you (remember the middle brother in the car when we first met saying "no, no, no"?) maybe you should entertain the warning. What if what they are saying is true?

♦ Not having sex too soon with a guy makes it so much easier to see the red flags clearly, and move on. Try this! You can thank me later.

JUST FRIENDS

My dealings with Cole, my so-called guy best friend, dated way back in time. In reality, we were much more than friends. Cole and I met on a blind date coordinated by my then male coworker, who happened to be his best friend. We met at Chili's for dinner and a "friendly" movie. Cole was cute, shorter than average, but dressed really nicely, attractive, overall handsome guy. He was a great conversationalist, asked many questions on our first date, and kept me entertained. There never was a dull moment.

Once we got into the movies, I noticed he was very much on the affectionate side—arm around shoulder, arm falling beside the waist. By the end of the movie, his hand was politely on the cusp of my behind.

Wow! He's an aggressive one, I thought.

By our second date, after our outing, he put the moves on even more, and we had ended up having sex in his apartment. From what I remember, it was pretty good, and that was that. It was so long ago, I don't really remember the intricate details. Besides I've shared so many, I don't think there is a real need.

Now what I do remember was that the very next day, while talking on the phone, discussing the fun we'd had the night prior, I said something about homosexuality that struck an absolute nerve with this guy. I forgot what was mentioned, but I do know that this brotha flew completely off the handle. He might have even cursed me out.

I went to work that Monday and told our mutual friend that it's obvious things aren't working out.

This fool said, "Well, he did mention the sex was good, Em."

"Gee, thanks, that makes it all better." As sarcastic as I sounded, deep down, in a very twisted place, that statement gave me a small amount of satisfaction.

♦

Moving forward many years, the same mutual friend and I had remained close. I would also see and hear about the best friend. Somehow, I'm not sure when, we made amends from that night and that was the onset of our own friendship.

Cole and I were that type of friends that, when we both weren't in a relationship, it was the perfect chance for us to kind of get together and have that companionship we both yearned for. For example, he would call me up to join him at a restaurant, using a Groupon he wanted to try, prior to taking a girl there, just to make sure it wasn't shady, and he wouldn't be embarrassed.

Or I would call him to get a man's opinion on a guy I was dating at the time, and would end up having a drink with him later that evening, things like that. You might ask, "What's wrong with having a friend of the opposite sex? This doesn't sound like a concern."

Well, it was.

I can recall many instances where our encounters could have or did actually cross the boundaries of the "friend zone." For instance, with the Groupon outing, by the end of the night, after having one too many drinks, we ended up kissing, and he performed oral sex on me in the car, before I managed to get out without him inviting himself up to my apartment.

Then I said casually, "We shouldn't be doing this, Cole. We are friends."

He agreed, I agreed, and it was a "see-you-when-I-see-you" type of thing.

Another instance, we hadn't seen each other in a while. He ended up getting a job in the same field I worked coincidentally, so we called ourselves going to happy hour to celebrate his new position and catch up. We had appetizers, a few rounds of drinks, and you guessed it, ended up making out before the night was over.

The next day he called and said, "Whoa! That got a little out of hand. You know I'm not looking for a relationship or anything, just started a new job, know what I mean?"

"Cole, shut up! No one is trying to date you. Calm down. Besides, we're just friends!"

He agreed, I agreed, and again, closing with "see-you-when-I-see-you".

♦

And there's more. My best friend and I were just hanging out one afternoon when Cole called and asked what I was doing. I told him, "I'm hanging out. What you doing?"

"Oh, me and my boy thinking about going to a strip club. You and Stacy wanna go?"

We both looked at each other like, *Strip club? That should be interesting. Maybe we can learn a few thangs.*

"Sure. Why not? We'll meet you up there."

So we sat, watched the strippers, laughed at him making serious conversation with them all, like he was on some speed-dating show, trying to really get to know them before giving them his money.

Now things got a little strange, because at some moments, instead of him looking at the strippers, his attention was on me.

I asked him a few times, "Hey, what's up? Are you drunk? What's your deal? All this ass around, why are you looking at me?"

"Man, you are just beautiful. I can't help it."

"Alright, Cole, whatever. You are tipsy and out of money. Let's wrap this up, okay? Besides, we are just friends."

However, there were two incidents over the time of our friendship that made me extremely uncomfortable about what we had.

My home girl Angel was getting married, and about fifteen of us girls were out in a limo ride to the latest nightclub for her final days prior to becoming the Mrs. It was the ultimate bachelorette party—lots of alcohol, some marijuana, and even ecstasy, which was new to me.

Not sure how I signed up for this, but my friend, the bride-to-be had never done any drugs before, I don't think, and was encouraged to spend her last days "feeling as good as possible."

So when someone slid her an ecstasy pill, she said, "Well, if Emily takes one with me, I'll do it."

Being the "good friend" I was, I said, "Sure, I'm down. Let's do this, Ang!" On the way out of the limo, I began to down my drink before entering the club.

One of our friends said, "Wait, you really don't need alcohol with X."

I responded, "No, I'll be fine!"

Guess what? I was not fine. What I remember of that night was that I kept having these blackouts, just going in and out of consciousness, even though I was moving around and functioning just fine. One minute, I would be at the bar with my girls, next minute I was on the dance floor.

Then I was in that long line waiting for a urinal. The one thing I kept telling myself was, *Perhaps I didn't need a drink after all, because this feeling is way out.*

So again, I had another blackout, and I was back on the dance floor, this time dancing with Cole. Yes, my friend Cole was at the same nightclub, on the same dance floor, and we somehow found each other and were dancing. I looked over and saw his best friend dancing with one of my home girls.

Let me tell you how this night was a little sketchy. Instead of driving home in the limo with my girls, Cole convinced me to take a ride with him in his brand-new BMW. I wanted to see the car anyway, so I guess it didn't take too much convincing. One of my girlfriends ended up coming along as well.

I had another blackout. When I woke up, I found myself at the gas station, where he was pumping gas.

My homegirl leaned forward from the back seat and said, "Wow! What's up with you and Cole?"

I told her, "What do you mean? This is my homeboy; we go way back."

"Yeah, right. It's obvious you guys have something going on. You two can't keep your hands off each—"

"No, we are just friends," Cole said, jumping back in the car.

Just friends, my behind.

Fast-forward to another blackout. I woke up this time at his condo, in the bathroom, on the commode.

"Cole, what the heck am I doing at your house? Where is Chanel?"

"Oh, I dropped her off at your girl's house. They had all just arrived in the limo."

I yelled from the bathroom, "Cole, my damn car is there, all my girls are there, how come you just didn't leave me with them?"

"Oh, well, you were super drunk, and I didn't want you to drive under those conditions."

Now I had about fifteen of my friends around me. If I was too drunk, I would have crashed at my girl's house with the rest of them.

I passed out for the last time and woke up, the next morning, luckily with all of my clothes on. Intoxicated and high out of my mind, I couldn't have told you what happened after I left his restroom that night. We could have had sex, or maybe we didn't;

I was always too embarrassed to ask. I knew I didn't belong there, not trusting that he was looking out for my best interest that night.

Well, unfortunately, I didn't learn my lesson that evening because I had several more interactions with him after that incident. Besides, he was my 'male best friend'. He came to all of my special events, award ceremonies, etc. I'd meet the chicks he dated, and even partied with him and a serious girlfriend he had over the years.

But the last straw was about five years after the bachelorette party scene.

♦

Remember, we now worked in the same industry, but my new position required some traveling. I was off to the Midwest for a three-day training, and guess who was scheduled for the exact same training? You guessed it—my guy BFF.

Things started off wrong from jump. He asked me if he could stay with me the last day of the training, so we could leave out the next day together for LA, saying it'll be a good time for us to catch up, since it had been about a year since we'd last hung out.

Right off the bat, I didn't think it was a good idea at all, so I kind of danced around the subject saying, "Well, we'll see."

Training time came, and here we were on the last afternoon of training, last night in the Midwest. My cell phone rang, and I answered it.

"Hey, where are you? What time will you be back in your room?"

"I'm here now actually," I said. "I was thinking, maybe you should just stay where you are at, so I can get a good night's rest, you can get a good night's rest, and we can just see each other at the airport."

"No, Em, stop being such a prude. We have the whole night to hang. Let's go to dinner, get a few drinks, and maybe hit up this local club I heard about during training. Come on, live a little."

"Ugh! Okay, okay."

"Hurry up! I'm hungry now, so I need a snack before dinner."

Cole was there in about ten minutes. We walked across the street to the local bar and had bar food and a beer. I told him all about my dating life, wanting to hear about his as well.

He said, "We need some real liquor to drink before we go out tonight."

Across from the hotel was a Costco, so we walked there to get alcohol—one big ol' pint of vodka and an economy-size cranberry juice. There was no way we could drink all of that in one night, but his idea was that we save money on drinks when we go out.

Fine. Whatever. "Let's just hurry up. It's going to take me a bit longer to get ready than you anyway."

I recall him making me a drink before I got in the shower. I took the drink with me. This was drink number two, since I'd had a beer earlier. I started to feel a buzz. I remember praying to God, *Please don't let me sleep with him. Let me make it through the night.*

Once I was dressed, I came out and was greeted with yet another drink.

"Drink up!" he said. "We'll go to Ruth Chris, and then we go to the club right after."

I thought to myself, *Perfect. I can suck up some of this liquor with a good filet.*

While applying my makeup as he was in the shower, my vision was becoming blurry. *Em, what are you doing? Why is Cole in there taking a shower? He shouldn't even be here. By now you know way better than this. Oh, if only you had put your foot down earlier.*

When I turned around, Cole was right behind me, wet, in a towel. Our eyes met, and before I can say, "What the heck are you doing? And why are you so close?" he kissed me. Just a small peck, but it was a sensual, deliberate, almost perfect peck on the lips. He moved away and proceeded to put on his clothes.

I knew right then that we were in for a very long night.

I remember shooting the breeze, laughing and joking in the back of the taxi, but super tipsy, like the drinks had snuck up on me extremely fast. As the door opened, it dawned on me that we were not at Ruth Chris. We were at that local club. It turned out to be a hole-in-the-wall club at that.

"Cole, how come we didn't go to eat?"

He said, "Oh, time kind of got away from us, so I just told the driver we would come here."

We walked in the place, and there weren't many of us in the club whatsoever. I really mean to say that we were the only Blacks there. To kill the awkwardness, we both ran straight to the bar.

Cole excused himself to the restroom. While he went and handled his business, I looked around, checking out my surroundings. I saw a couple of girls at the bar that seemed pretty friendly, so I started a conversation with them.

"Where are you from?" they asked. "Are you here for the training?"

"Of course, I am."

And things just kind of picked up from there.

I did notice that Cole was taking a rather long time in the restroom. I turned around and saw him in the corner talking to some girl. I walked over and told him, "Hey, my turn. I'll meet you here when I come out."

When I came out of the restroom, he wasn't where I told him I would meet him, but back at the bar, talking to the two girls I had just left.

So as I walked up, he immediately pulled me to the side. "Em, what did you say to those girls?"

"Nothing. We were just making small talk."

"Oh, okay. Well, when I got here, they were like, 'Hey, is that your friend? She is probably the prettiest black girl we've ever seen. Are you two a couple?' But I told them we're just friends."

I told him, "Hey, if you like them, talk to them."

So he kept up his conversation.

I glanced across the room and saw a few white boys staring my way. I'd always had a slight curiosity for white men, so I thought to myself, *You know what? I'm out of town, and there are a couple of Ryan Goslings over there looking my way. Why not? At least, I can talk to them, right?*

But first things first, I needed just a tad bit more liquid courage. "Bartender, another martini please."

Interlude

ROCK BOTTOM

I'm asleep, dreaming. No, I'm awake. My head was hurting something fierce. *What is that noise? Sounds like someone panting, out of breath. Better yet, what the heck is that smell?*

I opened my eyes and saw a dog—yes, a white, dingy, fluffy little dog—staring me right in my face. *But wait, I don't have a dog. As a matter of fact, I'm out of town in the freakin' Midwest. Where the heck did a dog come from?*

I jumped up, stepped back, and I immediately stumbled. As I felt my way around to catch my bearings, I noticed that clothes, trash, and paper cluttered the room. I suddenly felt nauseous and needed to throw up, so I ran out of the room, looking for the nearest bathroom.

The rest of the apartment was the same as the room where I woke up—dirty clothes everywhere, magazines, newspapers, food containers, with a sink full of dirty dishes. I made it to the restroom and leaned as far over the yellow-stained toilet as I could, with hair all over the place, trash, makeup, and hair gel, not to mention a dingy tub.

As I wiped my mouth and looked around this place, my heart started beating faster and faster, and my chest felt like it was caving in. *WHERE IN THE HELL AM I? Emily, calm down, breathe in and out, go back in the bedroom and figure things out.*

I headed back to the room, walking over everything on the floor. I had on socks, bra, and my sweater from the night before. No underwear, no pants. I got to the bedroom and saw Cole naked on the floor.

I kicked the mess out of him. "Get up, damn it!"

He jumped up startled.

"Cole, where in the hell are we? What happened?" I was trying my best to whisper because I heard snoring coming from the corner.

While Cole was getting up and putting on his clothes, I found the rest of mine and quickly put them on. I then walked over to the young lady who was sound asleep on the bed. She was white, brunette, and heavyset, about two hundred fifty pounds. She too was naked. I felt as if I was going to throw up again, as all the thoughts of what could have possibly happened that night ran through my mind.

Cole stumbled over something, trying to get to the bathroom, and woke her up.

"Oh, hey there," she said.

I didn't respond, I just stared at her.

"Hello. Emily, right? Are you okay?"

"No, she's not. She doesn't remember anything about last night," Cole said from the hallway.

"Wait, you mean to tell me you don't remember *anything?*"

They both chuckled.

I almost lost it right then and there but somehow managed to hold it together. "Let's get out of here, Cole. NOW!"

She walked us to the door, and I told Cole, "Give her some money."

"Give her some money? For what?"

I repeated, "Just give her some damn money." Why I insisted, I wasn't sure. It just felt like the right thing to do at the time.

We called a taxi, and we waited outside for it, for what seemed like the longest ten minutes of my entire life. Cole was talking, but I couldn't hear him at all. I was in a daze.

His words sounded like "Wha-wha-wha-wha-wha—"

"Cole, Cole, just be quiet." I was about to lose it again.

"You don't want to hear about last night?"

I told him, "I never want to hear about last night. Please don't ever speak to me about last night again in your life."

While in the taxi, we were dead silent.

It wasn't quite daybreak when we arrived back at the hotel, so he laid on the bed and crashed.

He said, "Let's get a few *Z*s before we have to catch our flight."

I still wasn't speaking to him. "Sure." I started packing. I just wanted out of there, and away from him. I wanted to hide away all alone to sulk in my guilt, shame, and misery.

While in the shower, I could have easily broken down, but I held it in. I didn't want him to see me broken. All the trust I had in this man was completely gone at this point.

♦

We were at the airport going through security, and he still wouldn't shut up. He finally got the hint to not discuss the night prior, but he felt like he just needed to have small talk, maybe to break the awkwardness between us. Who knows?

We flew different airlines, so I thought this was my chance to escape him and deal with my emotions. But he followed me to my gate and wanted to talk until my flight was ready to leave. Then he would walk to his.

I dealt with it for about fifteen minutes, and then he said the unspeakable.

Looking over at a pretty, slim white girl with long hair, he said, "See, Em, how come you couldn't pull a white girl like that for me? You had to get ol' fatty instead." He started laughing.

From that moment on, I hated him. I wanted him far, far away from me, or else I would have choked him out at that very moment.

Just then, an announcement came over the public address system: *"We will now begin boarding for Flight #1493 to Denver."*

"Well, it seems like you are about to board soon, so I will go on to my gate," he said.

As soon as he was out of sight, the tears started flowing down my face. They didn't stop the entire three-hour flight to my layover city.

Even while waiting to board my connecting flight, I couldn't stop crying. I was so overwhelmed by negative emotions- the guilt, the shame- that words can't fully describe how I was feeling. I couldn't help thinking how much worse that situation could have been. For me not to remember anything that happened that night, I could have woken up in shackles, beaten half to death, at the hands of a serial killer. Or I could have been raped by one of the men at the bar, or by several men, and left for dead in an alley.

Or even worse, I was still frightened by the possible details of what actually did happen that night.

I remember sobbing as my second flight took off. My seat mate politely asked me if I was okay.

I kindly answered, "No, far from it," closed my eyes, and started to pray. *"Lord, forgive me for I have sinned. I have done many things in my past, but this by far is the lowest. Please, Father, have mercy on me. Don't allow me to carry home with me any diseases. I pray that the pounding in my head stops soon, and that I sober up enough to look my children in the eye as they greet me at the airport."*

Then I went straight into a praise break. *"Lord, thank You for covering me even when I didn't deserve it. I could have easily been killed last night, but You saved me yet again. You have kept me, and if I have ever questioned Your presence, it is evident now that You have had me covered for years on end, and that it's obvious that You aren't through with me, Lord. If You find it in Your heart to forgive me, I will do whatever it is You want me to do from this moment on out. I will hear You, and I will listen. Your will and Your will only, Father. I'm yours in Jesus' name. Amen."*

I must've dozed off, because I woke up without any tears in my eyes. My heart was no longer heavy. I no longer felt guilty or shameful, and when I thought about Cole and the things that had happened the night prior, I no longer felt angry.

I whispered, *"Lord, You have forgiven me, therefore I forgive Cole. As a matter of fact, I can't even think about placing all the blame on him. I needed to have been strong enough to say no to him even coming to the room that night. You tugged at me all day, and I caved, I gave in to my flesh. I am the one responsible for last night. Praise God that I am forgiven."*

My relationship with Cole was never the same after that trip. We would see each other every so often, or text every now and then, but for sure, things were different. I never spoke to him about that trip again. I told very few people about what occurred, maybe only two or three. Now all of you know.

This was the hardest story for me to tell. However, I have no doubt that this will bless someone. It may or may not be you, but God specifically told me to include this, despite how controversial this story might be. I thought I would've felt shame, but I didn't. I thought I would've felt anxiety over publishing the story, but I don't. This is my story, and it was all a part of the learning process.

♦ There's no such thing as a friend you have sex with. Call it what it is…a homie lover friend, f* buddy, whatever.

♦ Drugs and alcohol almost always lead to bad judgment. Either just say no altogether, or never ever drink to excess.

♦ If you struggle with this…seek professional help. There's a very fine line between drug use, drug abuse and drug addiction.

♦ Do not accept drinks from any person who you don't fully trust. The few people who know about this incident, wondered if I was drugged. Just be mindful of this and be careful.

♦ Even when you hit rock bottom, God is still there. He is the just God as He was when times were good. Confess and repent of your sins and God can and will remove all guilt and shame.

♦ God is real, and He is our Protector. Enough said.

HE WILL RESTORE

God gave me another chance that day, and I made a vow to Him that I would do things differently from that day forward. I began to read my Bible every day and started a journal that consisted of reading Scriptures, understanding its concepts, and journaling based on the passage I had read that evening. I also had a book of prayers that I would look up and repeat out loud, based on the feelings I was having that day. For instance, if I was feeling guilty, I would look up prayers and scriptures pertaining to guilt. God spoke to me through His word and through my prayers. The more my relationship grew with the Lord, the more my conviction grew, prompting me to make a change in my life.

The first thing God brought to my attention was something that He had told me a long, long time ago. I must have been around twenty-three at the time, early for a change for church service, waiting on service to start. I sat in church listening to the gospel music that played over the speakers and just people-watched as members of the congregation came in.

I soon drifted off and started reminiscing about the wild

night I had had before with one of my little "shababies." A shababy was what I called a man that I did nothing but sleep with while I dated other potential mates.

Now before you even needed to know the definition of shababy, you probably wondered why in the world was I thinking about sex in church. Well, I'd had a good time the night before, so it ran across my mind.

I was just thinking about ol' boy and anticipating the next time I could see him again when a small, still voice said, *"Now, Emily, you know you are going to have to give up having sex out of wedlock."*

At this point, I was thinking, *I know that's not me talking.*

I heard the voice a second time.

"This is not what I have for you, daughter."

At that very moment, I knew it was God talking to me, so I talked back. "Ummmmm, no! Sorry, God. You will have to give me a pass on that one. Sex is too good. Besides, I don't lie, I don't cheat, and I am a nice, sweet person. I love my enemies. As a matter of fact, I love You Lord with all my heart, but um yeah, that's something I can't give up. Sorry. What else You got?"

I heard nothing after that, so I just figured, *Well, I told Him.* I kept on with my worship service that Sunday, kept on doing me, kept on having sex.

I heard the same voice saying the same thing several times after that day. I would say, at least once a year. In between relationships, I took a baby step and got rid of the shababies. They were no longer needed.

My problem would come up during times of being in a committed relationship. I just didn't know how to do it, to be honest. I would just say it with my mouth and not follow up with any action. So long story short, I kept failing at being celibate and eventually gave up.

Fast forward (after hitting rock bottom) to one day, I woke up with this overwhelming sadness, almost an instant depression. I thought to myself, *Why do I feel like this today? What the heck is going on?*

Then it dawned on me. It was my eldest daughter's fourteenth birthday, the age at which I lost my virginity with Mason, and after which I was having sex pretty consistently. Here I was, a single mother of two girls, telling them what the Bible says, "to wait until they are married to have sex," and I wasn't even practicing what I was preaching.

That was it. My driving force. Later that day, my daughter and I made a pact. That we would BOTH wait until we were married to have sex. We would honor our bodies and our temple and present them holy unto the Lord. A year later, on her fifteenth birthday, she made her own personal vow to God and sealed it with a promise ring that she bought herself. I wish I could tell you that everything was perfect for me after that day; it was not.

♦ Learn to hear and identify God's voice, and when you do, listen to it!

♦ We all have a choice. God gave that choice to us. Choose wisely.

♦ God is MERCIFUL and FAITHFUL. He never gives up on us! Just know that for yourself. He's right there waiting on us when we are ready to be obedient and submit ourselves to Him.

Chapter 10

HOW MANY DRINKS?

According to Matthew 9:17, "You can't put old wine in new wineskin or it'll break." Well, simply put, the moment I decided to become celibate, God identified other areas that I needed work on. So many areas. I was broken, and it was time to be healed before I was even remotely ready for Mr. Right.

I had been struggling with alcohol since fourteen or fifteen back when I lived in Arkansas in a foster home. That was how I coped with being away from my family, feeling a sense of abandonment from my immediate family in California, and even the distant relatives that lived in Arkansas. It didn't make sense to me why I was in a foster home when I had all these family members both near and far. Where was everybody? How come no one came to my rescue? I dealt with all of those emotions by self-medicating with alcohol.

As the years went by, I dealt with every issue I faced the exact same way. Tired of being single, I went drinking every chance I had with my girls. If I wanted to have fun with my new love interest, I went drinking. Stressed over my baby daddy, or a long day at work, I had a drink. It was my go-to drug for anything and everything.

Now a lot of people drink alcohol with no issues, but for me, it was an issue. There weren't too many times that I drank responsibly. I drank in excess to purposely get drunk. Having given thought to it, I realized that almost every one of my first sexual encounters with a new person involved having one too many drinks.

You recall that out-of-town experience where I hit rock bottom and woke up to that lady's nasty house? Well, as you know, that followed with an "I-am-never-drinking-again" moment. However, it wasn't until I became celibate did I realize how much of a stronghold alcohol had on me. So there were a lot of tough decisions I had to make in order to disassociate myself from alcohol. That meant no girls' nights out, no wine-tasting events, no happy hours, no clubs, and no birthday parties. My friends were not happy to say the least.

"How come you don't come outside anymore?" they'd ask.

"You no longer like to hang with us?"

I told them I was getting right with God and that I needed to control my drinking.

Then they'd say, "You don't have to get drunk. You're grown, we're grown."

They didn't understand. It's not that I didn't trust them, I didn't trust myself. I had to remove myself from those situations to avoid a relapse. I needed that isolation to regroup, to gain confidence that I could attend social events without going overboard. And I wasn't confident because I had failed too many times before.

For instance, for my thirtieth birthday, I had two events, an '80s party on Friday night, and a classy cocktail party the follow ing night at the W Hotel. My goal for my birthday weekend was to not get drunk, period. I wanted to remember the entire experience.

Not only did I not get drunk, but none of my close friends were drunk either. Look at God. My drinking buddies weren't even tipsy.

The second evening, I walked my last friend out to her car, went in the house, wrapped my hair up, took my makeup off, took a shower, lay down, and reflected on what an amazing thirtieth birthday weekend I had just experienced.

That had never happened before in my life. My past birthday celebrations consisted of waking up with all of my clothes on, and sometimes not, calling my best girlfriends and asking them, "Where is my car? How did I get home?" So, yes, that was a win for me.

Disappointment soon followed. The third night was a Sunday, and it was my good friend, Ashbinah's birthday bash, held at a popular nightclub in LA. The birthday girl had VIP bottle service, all of my best girls were going, and it was guaranteed to be a star-studded event. Ash always did it big, so it was something I didn't really want to miss.

I was exhausted from my two birthday parties, and honestly, something in my gut told me not to go, to be content with my pair of wins over the weekend. But out of fear that I would disappoint my friend, and would miss out on an epic night, I went anyway, tired and drained as I was.

As you can guess, I woke up the next morning with all of my clothes and makeup on from the night before, hungover like nobody's business. I peeked outside to see if my car was in the driveway, and then I rushed to take my daughter to school because we had already missed her bus.

On the drive back home, I called into work. I then called Ash, the birthday girl.

She answered, "Oh my God, Em—"

I hung up immediately, not wanting to know what happened after the last round of tequila shots. I had snippets of the night prior, none of which I even wanted to remember the full details, so I suppressed those memories.

For about two to three weeks, I avoided all of my friends, until finally I called Ash specifically to get the details of the night.

Long story short, I wasn't happy with the report—an epic fun night for my friends and an epic fail for me.

It took some time, completely removing myself from alcohol for a minute, just to get my bearings. Over time, I was able to go to functions and strictly adhere to my new two-drink maximum. No matter what the occasion, two drinks, if any, was it for me. That limit remains to this day.

Lessons Learned

♦ Although removing sex was the goal, God also revealed to me yet another stronghold associated with this activity, for me this was alcohol.

♦ Ask God what *your* stronghold might be. Sex, alcohol, drugs, low self-esteem, past abuse. Whatever *it* is...God can and will remove it.

♦ When he shows it to you, listen. Be obedient. Be ready to break that chain, expeditiously.

♦ God will continue to work on you, and work on you, until you are in position for His ultimate will. So just sit back and enjoy the ride. (OK that was too much, you probably won't enjoy it, however, this is crucial to the journey. Embrace the process).

MAKE ME OVER

So now I was at the point of being celibate and sober (I use this term loosely, but you get my drift) and was patting myself on the back for doing well in these two areas. Then *Bam!* God hits me with more. One day while shopping in the mall at one of my favorite stores, the sales clerk called me by name. I had recognized her too but didn't expect her to call me by my government name, as if she knew me, in front of all these people. It hit me right then and there—I had replaced having a man and having sex with good ol' shopping.

I went home that evening and just did a tour around the house. Not only were my closets filled with new clothes, shoes, and bags, but both of my girls' closets were filled as well. Then I sat down and looked at my infamous budget sheet. I did a tally of my credit card balances. Sure enough, all of them had sky-rocketed. I knew then, God was revealing to me that I needed to get my finances in order.

By this time, I had about 100K worth of credit card, installment, and student loan debt. Every year I would promise to start paying that debt off. I considered filing bankruptcy, but a financial advisor made it loud and clear, "You are not destitute, so get your bills together and pay them. Simple as that."

So that's what I did. I gathered all my bills, cut up all my credit cards, and put myself on a budget. I set aside a certain amount to pay off my bills and started paying them down nice and slow. On this new budget, I could no longer buy a new outfit every time I went out on a date or to an outing. I had about $25 a week of walking-around cash to work with (you heard right, $25 a week). I paid my tithes faithfully and I managed. My daughters were sad because we went to the park on the weekends, instead of the mall. The entire house had to make adjustments, but we did it.

In order to bring more cash in, I decided to focus on moving up in my position at work. Working long hours, I explained to my management team that I wanted to be promoted and asked exactly what I needed to do to get there. I did what they said. I also cranked our side hustle, a tax business that had been in our family for years. I worked hard, I made money, and I reduced my expenses, including trading my Mercedes-Benz in for a Honda Accord. I also mixed and matched outfits, and wore the heck out of my designer bags, instead of putting them away for special occasions. Every day was a special occasion because I knew I wasn't buying any more anytime soon. And I got caps replaced on my stiletto heels, instead of buying new ones.

In addition to finances, there were a few other spring cleaning things I had to buckle down and do. I completed a master's thesis that I had spent the last five years dragging my feet on. I took another period of isolation, knocked out the thesis, crossed the stage, and got my master's degree.

I also wanted to lose weight, so I cut back on my eating, worked out consistently, and lost twenty pounds (probably for the third time now). Clean up work was happening all around me, work I had neglected because I was spending so much time in and out of wrong relationships, chasing love. God said it was time to complete the things that I'd started, so I completed them. God said it was time to get my house in order, so I cleaned house. He was in the process of making me over.

♦ My first move was to get closer to God, by reading my bible daily, praying, journaling and even fasting at times.

♦ Then God made his move, by showing me little by little, major things that I had to change in order to be the woman of God he had created me to be.

♦ The difference this time, I listened and obeyed him, at every nudge, at every pull. I was desperate for Him, and wide open to his direction.

♦ Ask yourself, or better yet, ask God, what things do you need to do for him to make you over? Write those things down as he reveals them to you, take action immediately, and give God the glory as you cross those tasks off your list.

♦ Here's to the new you!

Chapter 12

SUPERPOWER

So now that I had a few things in order, I felt it was time to start dating again. I first asked God how to present myself differently. I wanted a different experience, I no longer wanted to repeat the same mistakes that I did in the past. Again, I asked God where to start, and before bringing men back into my life, there were still changes that I needed to make. *Good Lord! What do you have up your sleeve now...* "This time, you are doing things MY way", is what he told me. Below is what that looked like for me. If you are curious of what 'dating God's way' may look like, here's a good time to take your pen and paper out to take notes.

My attire had to change: Remember my college friend, Giovanna? Anyway, her dad is the coolest dad ever. He's younger, a little flirty at times, but nonetheless, he tells it like it is. Visiting my friend's dad one afternoon, the three of us were having a conversation, and I was explaining to him that I was celibate, and willing to date again, but it seemed like I was only attracting perverts. I couldn't figure out why these men were even approaching me.

"Did they not see the God in me?" I asked. "Do they not notice that I am in my spiritual realm?"

He answered, "No, they don't. You know what they see?"

I responded, "No. What do they see?"

He said, "They see sex. Though you're celibate, you still have sex written all over you. You always have. Heck, if I were twenty years younger, I would try to talk to you myself."

I stood up, looked across the room in the floor-length mirror and it was like the light bulb went off. It was summer time, and I had a long maxi dress on, but my "girls" were all out. As a matter of fact, I often had my girls out all the darn time. They were my pride and joy, my best asset, natural double Ds. Women in Hollywood paid good money for these. I used to think, *Why not flaunt them?*

I was thankful for Pop's brutal honesty that day. If I wanted to attract a different type of guy, I had to put the girls away. I took it a step further and bought bigger clothes. Just because I could fit a size six didn't mean it wasn't tight, so I went back to what was comfortable, which was size eight. I threw or gave away dresses and blouses that showed too much cleavage. And my signature date-night outfit went from skintight bandeau dresses with cleavage out to a nice pair of jeans, blouse, and cute heels with everything covered up. I played up my hair, jewelry and light make up, instead of flaunting my curves. My goal was to leave something to the imagination. It worked. I eventually stopped attracting perverts.

My attitude toward men had to change: I had to get rid of the idea that all men were cheaters and liars. I held on to the notion that the man God had ordained for me would also be celibate, honest, fully available to me, and that there were some good Christian men out there. I didn't know where they were, but I knew they were out there. I wanted to get married to one of them. I wrote these very same words on a piece of paper, taped them to my mirror on my dresser, and repeated them daily. I chanted my ideal guy, over and over again, until I believed he was out there. I also treated every man that I had met with that same respect, as if it was him. Until he proved himself otherwise. I found the good in every man I met. Pretty soon, I started having true respect for men, something I had lost along the way.

My disposition towards men changed: Once my attitude changed, and men had re-earned my respect, I started looking at men through an entirely different lens. When I was out, I smiled more at them. If I noticed a man watching me from across the room, I smiled, gave a nice nod, and went on about my business. When I was approached, I was warm, welcomed most, engaged in the conversation, and offered a compliment or two if they were dressed nice or smelled good or had a nice smile. Men were no longer the enemy, out to get my cookies, out to play me. No, they were now men, a guy I had just met, who had a nice smile, or had on a pair of nice shoes. I liked men, I respected them, I no longer prejudged them.

My confidence was on 10. I hear women say so many times, "No one approaches me. I go out all the time, and I don't meet anyone." I found that to be so far from the truth, the moment I stopped thinking negatively about myself. The moment I started seeing men as humans, potentially good people, and harmless because I was a queen, empowered and could choose to entertain them or not. They were no longer a threat to me, and I was no longer a threat to them.

Everywhere I went, I looked good, hair done, nails done, everything done. Why? This made me feel more confident, and that same confidence attracted men toward me. There wasn't a single night out with my girls, not one single barbeque, grocery store run, or gym run when I wasn't approached by someone. Mind you, I was now dressing very modestly. I looked for the good in every man that approached me and decided if they were "good enough" for a date with the New Em. If not, I politely said "thank you" for whatever compliment they gave, and kept it moving.

My idea of dating changed: What is dating? What is it meant for? What God revealed to me was that dating is simply a friendship where you spend time with another person in order to figure out if you want to marry them. Simple as that. It's not for casual sex, and it's not for playing house or acting as if you are married. It's that time when you try to get to know someone, to see if you share common interests.

Once I took sex out of dating, everything was better. I was more confident, I dated with purpose, and my judgment was no longer clouded. I didn't have to ask for ten different opinions when I felt something was wrong. It was as if God was coaching me through the dating process the whole time, like live feed in an earpiece. *"No daughter, not him. Move on."*

I followed God's lead, and when he said move on, I did. This time, there was no second-guessing, no clouded judgment from good sex, or competition with the next chick. I knew what I wanted, and if he didn't fit the mold, it was on to the next.

I was finally OK with being single: Dating God's way makes you an expert at finding out what you do like and what you don't. If I dated a man who spent his waking hours and late nights on Facebook and Instagram liking this girl's pictures and that girl's bikini photos, or being tagged in pictures with his arm wrapped around another female, talking about that's his friend, then I'm good. I would tell them that this isn't going to work out. If they asked why, then I would explain. Then, of course, they would try to make me feel insecure, explaining that it's not such a big deal, and that's really his home girl from college. "No worries, this just isn't going to work. I'm looking for something different." This went for men who did not meet my criteria, anytime I saw red flags, anytime I felt as if *he's not the one.* I wanted what I wanted and wasn't afraid of being alone until I got it.

I embraced courtship: I didn't like doing a lot of work in relationships. In fact, I hated it. I received no satisfaction from doing all of the work. At some point, I learned that you give to receive. In past experiences, I treated and treated and treated and hardly got anything in return, except "Thank you, babe," or "You are so sweet."

I later figured out that men actually like to pursue women, and I simply started letting them. The first few dates, I would usually meet at our destination, just to be safe. But after the second or third date, I allowed them to pick me up outside my home. I hesitated at the door for him to open my car door for me. I didn't lay down the law on our first few dates, talking about I like this, I like that, and you have to do this and that for me. No, I simply let my actions speak. So, yes, I hesitated before opening the car door and politely waited for it to be opened for me. Same with the door to the restaurant or anywhere we were going—slight pause, wait for the door to be opened, and gently walk through with a smile and a thank you every time.

I never picked up the tab. No "oh-I-got-it-this-time," nothing. My thought is, you're courting me, trying to win my love, not the other way around. The waitress would set it down, and I never even looked that direction. My eyes stayed fixed on my companion for the night as I continued with our conversation. I would thank him for such a lovely dinner and comment on what I liked most about the dinner, be it conversation, food, or atmosphere, and kept it moving.

If a guy asked me what I liked to do for fun, I told him. In time, men would take me to those places. When my birthday and Valentine's Day came around and they asked me what I liked, sure enough, I'd get it. I never had to spend a dime or give up the "cookie."

I'm telling you, I was having a great time dating. Men did nice things for me, and I verbally expressed how much I appreciated it. Next thing I knew, they were doing something else nice for me. *Who knew things worked this way?* I no longer thought the single life sucked. Had I known how wonderful this would be, I would have stopped having sex a long time ago. My confidence was way up. I enjoyed the weeding out process, and I was enjoying being courted. This was a breeze.

God became my ultimate advisor: OK, so yes, I was having a ball being courted. However, it wasn't about fun. I wanted to be a wife. I wanted to find my husband. So every guy I dated, I would pray before our date "God, reveal to me if this is the one". Sometimes, during the date, same prayer. After every date, you guessed it, same prayer. Because of this, dating moved very quickly for me. Average length before God told me "no" was about 3 dates. Sure enough, I would start seeing red flags, inconsistencies, their representative revealed. Not to say something was wrong with him, he just didn't align with my ideal guy, for whatever reason. I would ask God, and soon enough, he would show me. He was my relationship coach, and if I were to be successful, I would have to listen. Although the one hadn't shown himself yet, things were great.

I must admit, though, school wasn't over for me just yet. I knew things were too good to be true. I still had some learning to do, celibate and all.

♦ Wow, God really showed me at this point how dating was supposed to be done.

♦ Part of the main superpower was finally allowing men to lead! They asked for my number first, they initiated the call or text, they asked me out on a date, they paid for dinner, etc. I followed their lead. I allowed them to pursue me.

♦ This process may look different for you. However, I highlighted the main few that I think could be applicable to most. Best thing to do is to ask God specifically for your very own masterplan.

♦ Had I known removing sex from dating would result in this much fun, I would have listened to God a long time ago. That's it…carry on.

Chapter 13

BILLS, BILLS, BILLS

I had acquired a "superpower" with my new dating techniques that I put into practice, along with my celibate lifestyle. But things sort of got out of hand, and God had to check me immediately. Here's the tea.

I was first introduced to a man by one of my coworkers during a casual conversation about party planning. I was planning an event and was looking for a nice, classy venue. At that time, I had already started getting my finances in order and funds were well budgeted. I didn't have enough money for the type of event I was trying to pull together, without using credit, which was a no-no at that point in my financial rehabilitation process.

I said to my coworker jokingly, "This is one time when a sponsor would come in handy." A sponsor is what you would call a guy who had money and didn't mind spending it on you, usually with no strings attached. They may or may not have other women, and if they did, it really didn't matter. At this point, I had only heard of sponsors. Now don't go judging me for all of a sudden being interested in a sponsor, because at first it was a joke.

My coworker responded, "I have a sponsor for you. I could

introduce you," and proceeded to tell me about a guy she used to work with, who dated younger women and would treat them all the time. Of course, my interest piqued.

At first I just laughed at the story, thinking, *This can't be real. Where do guys like this exist?*

A little while after our conversation was over, I glanced at my budget sheet with my negative red figures in parentheses, looked back at my coworker, back at budget sheet, and finally said, "Hey, girl, why don't you go ahead and hook that up?"

Before I knew it, a very nice man well into his forties was at my door to pick me up for our first date. I have to admit, I had reservations from the start. Yes, the age difference between us was the largest gap I'd ever had with someone I dated. And just from the first time seeing him, I knew the physical attraction was just not there.

He dressed neatly and was well groomed. But some men will tickle your fancy, and some won't. He didn't tickle mine. He was about five seven, had more weight on him than I tend to like, his hair was graying, and he wore glasses. My idea of dating an older man would be having the smooth, deep-voice, tall, dark, and handsome actor, Dennis Haysbert, on my arm (Whitney's lover in *Waiting to Exhale*). Or the internet sensation #mrstealyour-grandma. So this guy definitely missed the mark on my "older-dude-attractiveness scale."

He quickly redeemed himself by being a perfect gentleman, opening doors for me and pulling out my seat. We talked and laughed and were having a great conversation.

Then he said, "So tell me more about this event you are planning."

I replied, "Well, I've found the perfect venue, but it's beyond my budget. I still need to continue looking, but I'm running out of time. I might even have to cancel if I don't find something soon."

He paused, took a bite out of his steak, looked up, and asked, "Well, how much are you short?"

"Oh, just five hundred dollars."

He paused again and took another bite. "That's not bad. I can cover that."

I couldn't help thinking, *Wow! My coworker was right. That was way too easy. We're only halfway through our first date.* "Wait, are you serious? Because, if you are, that would be fantastic. It'll be a huge help. You would be practically saving my entire event."

Needless to say, he gave me the money, I had my event, and we had a great time. I hate to admit, I didn't even invite this man to the party, which later had hurt his feelings. That was the first time I hurt him, but not the last.

I spent months after that trying to make up for not inviting him. I did this by engaging in conversations, going out on dates with him, basically being a pretty young female companion to him. Eventually he grew on me, and turned out to be one of the nicest guys I've ever met. We could talk for hours and hours and hours.

He'd confide in me about his relationship problems, and I would give him advice from a female's perspective. But I knew for a fact that this man was interested in me, and I tried my best to dance around any conversation about us seriously dating. I mean, our friendship was growing and we were having a good time, but my reservations about the physical attractiveness remained the same. He couldn't understand why our relationship didn't get off the ground.

I didn't want to let him go, since I liked the friendship and the nice dinners and the occasional cash he provided me. One evening I kissed him good night after he walked me to the door. That simple peck gave me three to four more months with him. Soon he became my "oldie-but-goodie."

One day while visiting him at his house, I mentioned, "I could use a mini-vacation."

He asked, "Well, where do you want to go?"

I didn't have a clue.

He started naming a few local spots in California, and eventually we decided on Santa Barbara. I had never been, so I thought it would be a nice trip. He did all of the planning, and we were all set to leave the next weekend.

Once he arrived to pick me up and before getting my bag, he glanced up at me and said, "Wow! You are stunning. I cannot wait for this weekend to begin."

Just the glow in his eyes at that very moment made my stomach turn. I thought, *Uh-oh, I hope he doesn't think he's getting any this weekend.*

We took the three-hour drive and pulled up to the most beautiful hotel I'd ever been to. Parked out front were Bentleys, Porsches, Maseratis, giving you an idea of the clientele.

Our suite looked like a cute little cottage you would see in the movies. It had two double doors that opened up to the most gorgeous view of the Pacific. He had a dozen roses and a bottle of champagne waiting for me with a note: HERE'S TO THE BEST-WEEKEND YOU EVER HAD.

He apologized on behalf of the resort, since there were no more double beds left, only single king-size beds.

Yeah, right. But it didn't matter. I loved the room, the resort, and everything else about that place. I was in heaven.

We did the typical resort stuff, relaxed in a private cabana, even saw Bradley Cooper at the pool. He swore up and down that the actor was checking me out. To this day, I'm still flattered by that. Then we went on a long scenic walk, an outdoor movie, dressed up, and had a beautiful dinner. Nighttime came and we made our way back to the room. I could already tell he was getting ready to put on the moves.

After I showered, I put on my homely cotton two-piece pajama set, jumped right in bed, and said, "Good night. Today was great," and went right to sleep. I didn't even look at him, but I could've felt the disappointment from the other side of the bed.

♦

The next morning during breakfast I could tell he was upset. I tried not to mention anything to trigger an argument. As I went back to the room to change to get ready for my scheduled spa appointment, I suddenly felt a little sad, seeing all the couples hugged up. I felt empty, a little envious, and felt like I was missing out.

My massage was fantastic. Just what I needed. I hadn't had a man touch me in a long time and although this was just a full body massage, I was relaxed and thoroughly enjoyed all of the sensual touches. I remember thinking, completely in my flesh at the moment, *I wish I had a real boyfriend here with me this weekend. A* real *boyfriend?* That's when I knew and finally admitted to myself that I was using oldie-but-goodie. I knew I wasn't attracted to him, and I had spent months of his time, my time, and most importantly, his money to my advantage. And that really wasn't fair. After my massage, I told myself that I was going to give him a real shot.

We went out later that evening, and I dressed up really cute for him, like I would have if he was my real man. I was very affectionate during dinner, holding hands, glancing in his eyes. When we got back to the room, I thought, maybe we can kiss again, and talk, and I can let my guard down a little, just to see if it was just my stereotyping him as being older or if it was something I could deal with.

Despite my best efforts, I couldn't fake being attracted to him when I clearly wasn't. I had an exact repeat of the night before.

♦

On the drive home, oldie-but-goodie was silently fuming in the driver's seat. I finally asked him, "What's wrong?"

He let me have it. "You let me spend all my money this weekend when clearly you don't want to be with me."

I asked, "Why you say that?" wondering what exactly gave me away.

"You know why I said that. You were so close to the edge of the bed last night, if I gave you the slightest nudge, you would have fallen face down on the floor."

I chuckled at just the thought, but he did not. His face was downcast, no longer mad, but clearly his self-esteem had been affected by my selfishness.

I don't recall if we had the conversation that night or a few days later, but I finally admitted to oldie-but-goodie that things weren't going to work out between us, that I didn't want a relationship with him. *Lord, forgive me for using oldie-but-goodie. I took your new skills you taught me for granted and I promise never to do this again.* This was the first time I had prayed about him, during this entire time we dated.

♦ Don't use men, period. It's not cool, it's ungodly, and it's hurtful to the other party.

♦ You can tell if you are physically attracted to someone, even without having sex with them. It's called chemistry, and chemistry is important. If you find it lacking in a potential partner, it's best to just let that person go.

♦ Your new superpowers are great, but please don't use them inappropriately.

♦ Dating is for information, an interview grace period for a potential life partner. If there is something that disqualifies that person, that doesn't really connect with what you are looking for, let them know as soon as possible. Don't prolong it. Save yourself time, and don't waste that man's time either. Remember, karma is a beast.

Chapter 14

ON TO THE NEXT ONE

Well, I continued to serial-date, basically going through my weeding-out process, hanging out with my girls in the meantime. At this point, Camille was my ultimate hangout buddy. She was always on the go, a true social butterfly, and at every opportunity, I went along with her. We had girl-nights-out, sleepovers, we traveled, attended events, whatever came up, she was my main partner-in-fun. A lot of the times, we would hang out with her boyfriend and his group of friends. They were a lively crew and we always had a good time with those guys.

One afternoon, Camille called and told me that one of her boyfriend's friends had inquired about me from a picture posted on Facebook. You know how social media hookups go, so of course I wasn't exempt.

I looked him up, and the guy was actually cute, which was a plus. When he sent me a message asking to take me out, I thought, *Why not?*

"Are you Brandon?" I asked as I walked in the restaurant and quickly saw his familiar face from his Facebook profile.

"Yes, it's me," he responded. "Pleasure to meet you."

Just a few minutes in to our first date, I immediately noticed something different about him. He was a little on the proper side, the way he talked, even his mannerism, so I could tell he was raised around very few blacks. Sure enough, he was born and raised in Torrance, CA, in a predominantly white neighborhood. He enjoyed activities I wasn't used to, like snowboarding, dirt biking, and cycling. I found him very…interesting.

We got to know each other more and more. I explained that I was celibate and waiting for marriage, which he found admirable, like all men did, and he said that wouldn't be a problem with us dating. He was a nice guy. I couldn't find too much wrong with him, not that I was looking, but there weren't too many red flags initially. He had a daughter a year younger than my elder daughter, and she seemed to be his world. I admired that. (Good dads are always attractive to single moms). He was gentleman-like and a foodie (what my inner fat girl loved the most about him), and so far, I was enjoying his company.

We dated for about a month or so, and often double-dated with my BF and her man. I remember thinking to myself, *Okay, this is cool. He's different than what I am used to, but in a good way. I think I like this guy.* And hearing my best friend's man say that he talks about me all the time, that he's never seen his friend like this with anyone only added fuel to the fire.

Now at this point I was getting a bit uneasy. You see, this was the very first time that I actually liked a guy I was dating, and hadn't seen any red flags yet after about four dates and seeing each other pretty consistently for six weeks or so.

I remember thinking, *Now what? I like him, he likes me. How do we continue dating AND be celibate?* This was new to me. But I decided that I'd just play it by ear.

♦

One evening, he got off work late, the girls were with their dads that weekend, and I was home alone. It was about nine thirty when he called and asked, "What you up to?"

"I'm relaxing."

"Do you want me to come over, since you're kid-free? We can watch a movie, have a drink or something."

Right then, my gut told me that it probably wasn't a good idea, but then that other voice, my flesh, my desire to have male company especially during a kid-free weekend, snuck in. "Sure, come on over."

He arrived with a brown paper bag in his hand.

"What you got in that bag?"

"I heard you like Hennessy."

Hennessy, darn it, was "my kryptonite." I guess my friend's boyfriend spilled the beans. I thought to myself, *I'll just have one drink.*

That one drink led to two, and although I hadn't gone over my two-drink limit, I was more intoxicated than I wanted to be. Especially with a man that I liked, in my living room, on my couch.

I'm not sure what movie we were watching at the time, but there had to have been a scene with some type of sexual undertone. Having had my liquid courage, I said, "Well, I know you've had your share of white girls." Considering he had been raised around a lot of white people.

"What do you mean?"

"Sexually."

"Well, I guess you can say that. Why do you ask?"

"Well, is it true?"

"What?"

"That they are the best headmasters?"

He laughed uncontrollably. "I can't believe you just said that."

Then I said, "Well, are you going to answer the question?"

He turned around and looked me dead in the eye. "No, absolutely not. Not even close."

For whatever reason, his dismissal right in front of me of the old myth of white girls being better in bed than black women triggered all of my suppressed loins and was an immediate turn-on.

As you can imagine, one thing led to another, and my celibacy streak had ended, just like that, over two glasses of Hennessy and talk of Becky with the good hair.

♦

We went out for brunch the next day. I reiterated to him that I still wanted to wait until I got married, explaining that I'd had a little too much to drink and made a bad choice the night before.

He kind of rolled his eyes in the back of his head but then agreed that we would keep trying the "no-sex thing," as he called it.

As you can imagine, over the next month there were all sorts of red flags going off with this guy. His love for his daughter sounded almost like an obsession to me. I would take him to a restaurant he hadn't been before, we would enjoy it, and then he would be right at that restaurant the next day with his daughter. Or if he had her for the weekend, he rarely called, and when he did, he would tell me all the cool things they did together over the weekend.

But when it came to our weekend, he'd ask me, "Well, what do you want to do today?" That's even if we had a weekend. He wasn't used to having a girlfriend, so the weekends outside of having his daughter usually consisted of catching up on sleep, sleeping for ten to twelve hours straight. After his long nap, he would call me over to his house, which may or may not have led to sex, but definitely would have led to inappropriate behavior.

The lack of consistent calling and the mere fact that we weren't taking celibacy seriously started to become too much for me. I was beginning to feel like he was just waiting for me to slip up. I confirmed with praying to God one night and immediately got enough nerve to go over to his house and let him down easy. At least, I thought I did. I explained that I didn't think we were right for each other, and the next person that comes along, he should treat her the way he treats his daughter.

The man turned red in the face, started punching the wall. I could tell he was trying very hard not to cry. I actually started getting scared and made my way toward the door. I couldn't figure out why he reacted that way. I figured he wouldn't even care.

Well, that wasn't the end of us. Considering we had mutual friends, we both had friends in our ear saying that we should work it out, that we're so cute together.

So, in short, he came back and asked for another chance, saying he would get better with spending time, and was okay with the celibacy.

That second chance lasted for an entire year. We had a few slip-ups sexually, at least four over that period. Going back and forth with wanting to be celibate took a toll on him, which was totally understandable.

I met his mother after I kept complaining that I had introduced him to my entire family and friends, yet I had only met his daughter. He also took me to the house of a childhood friend to meet his family. He took me snowboarding, an epic fail for me, but he turned it into a cool video of bloopers that I was able to share with my friends. I got used to his dry sense of humor.

I loved him, I did. And yes, he did court me like a gentleman. Considering this was my first real, committed relationship since my new superpower, I noticed over time that I did want to treat him sometime. To show my appreciation. I would cook dinner for him, by little gifts here and there, cologne or whatnots. Treated him out to a nice dinner for his birthday. Things were going good. We toasted our one-year anniversary with, "One year down, many more years to go!"

Because we were making good progress on the issues that I did have with him, I could have easily settled to be with this man. But there was still something missing about him, missing from us. It wasn't the head-over-heels experience I was looking for.

He did start going to church with me sometimes, although he hadn't been to church in years. His mother was ecstatic about him getting back into the church and re-establishing his relationship with Christ, which he gave me credit for.

A couple of months after our one-year anniversary, things were just not coming together like I had hoped. I couldn't really put my finger on it; I just knew deep down that I wanted more. Maybe the fact that he did not want more kids could have contributed to the way I felt. I told him I was indifferent, when in fact,

I really did want to try for a son, and was hoping that he would come around. I had a good feeling that his daughter was good enough for him. I also didn't know how my own daughters would come into play. He loved his own daughter so much, it didn't seem like there was any room for my two.

After factoring all of this in, I finally got enough nerve to leave him. When I did, he begged and pleaded and asked what he needed to do to make things right. I told him nothing, that it was me, not him.

He sent a Louis Vuitton gift card to my job that was enough for a nice-sized purse. Although he definitely knew a way to a girl's heart with money for a new handbag, I had to stay strong.

I kindly drove to his place, and returned the gift card back to him. That day outside his apartment, I remember my heart sinking when he asked, "What did I do?"

In reality, he didn't do anything major. It just wasn't right, and I needed to be bold enough to let him go. That was our last encounter, the day we had broken up.

A few months later, I got word from our friends that he was in the hospital for hypertension, closely related to the strenuous work on his job. Once I found out that it wasn't critical, I didn't go to see him, opting to send flowers instead. I didn't want to see him. I needed to stand firm that God was telling me that he was not the one. Had I stayed in a desperate place, and only wanted to be married, instead of God's best for me, I would have continued to date him, and we may have been married by now. I'm almost certain of it.

Lessons Learned

♦ When you are practicing celibacy and you decide to enter into a committed relationship with someone, clear, concrete boundaries will have to be established from start (discussed later in the book). As you saw in this case, without the boundaries set, failure was inevitable.

♦ Testing the waters (sexually) should not be of importance. I'd rather you KNOW that he/she is the one, than KNOW that the sex is good still wondering if he/she is for you. (again, in my case here).

♦ It doesn't take drama, or something drastic to happen, to know when a man is not for you. Follow your gut. If you don't trust that, simply ask God "Is this man for me?" He'll show you if he's not.

♦ If God says no, be ready to obey, move on, and do not be swayed otherwise by friends, family or your own imaginary clicking clock. God's best should be your goal, not just good enough.

♦ When God says no, it's on to the next. Just like that.

Chapter 15

BUTTERFLIES

On my thirty-second birthday, I received a text message at exactly midnight (two a.m. his time) from Devin, my ex from Arkansas turned good friend. We had kept in contact over the years, even after the "I'm-having-a-new-baby" incident. Although our talks weren't as frequent after that, when they did happen, they were fantastic.

I responded to his text: WHY ARE YOU UP SO LATE?

He responded:I WANT TO BE THE FIRST PERSON TO WISH YOU HAPPY BIRTHDAY

Well, I let him know he'd succeeded, and we left it at that. About a week later, we texted each other, and he asked how my relationship with Brandon was doing. I told him not so hot (this was prior to our breakup) and that things just weren't sitting well with me.

His response was: EM, JUST PRAY ABOUT IT AND SEE-WHAT GOD THINKS

So that's exactly what I did.

Two weeks later, I received another text from Devin again. Mind you, this was unlike him. Usually it would take months before hearing from him again, sometimes even years. We exchanged small talk, and he casually asked: WHAT DID YOU DECIDE ABOUT OLD DUDE

I responded: I'M STILL DECIDING

OK COOL. LET ME KNOW HOW THINGS WORK OUT

Two weeks after that, I received yet another text from Devin. I knew he was up to something. *Now if he asks me about Brandon one more time, I know for sure he is fishing around.*

He texted: WHAT DID YOU DECIDE ABOUT OLD DUDE

I replied, WE BROKE UP MAYBE A DAY OR SO AFTER WE LAST CHATTED. I PRAYED ABOUT IT, AND IT JUST WASN'T RIGHT

Then there was a long pause before he texted back, CAN I CALL YOU?

My heart started pounding. I did so much better talking with him via email or text. Besides, it was late. *What does he want to talk about?* Eventually, I put my "big-girl panties" on and allowed him to call.

♦

The last time I had seen Devin was about five years prior when I went to Arkansas to handle some family business due to my mom being ill. We'd met in the lobby of the hotel I was staying and talked for hours. At that time, I was dating Sebastian, the pretty boy from work. I showed him pictures and everything of my new man, and he talked about the women he was dating.

We walked around the hotel lobby for a bit, and as I turned, I found him standing pretty close, in my personal space, looking dead in my eyes. I could have gotten lost right there in that very moment. Suddenly, I was awash with feelings I hadn't felt in years. I had a sudden urge to just move in closer and get one of his passionate hugs and sweet forehead kisses while I closed my eyes and exhaled. I exhaled anyway, taking two steps away from him. I smiled, and then so did he. I shook it off (in my mind) and proceeded to the elevator.

Time to go, Devin, I said to myself. *Time to go.*

He walked me up to my room, and we said our goodbyes.

The following day, as I was leaving the city, I sent him a text thanking him for coming by the night prior and mentioned how it was so good to see each other. I texted: NOT SURE WHAT IT IS, BUT IT SEEMS AS THOUGH GOD LEFT US WITH SOMETHING SPECIAL ALL OF THESE YEARS.

He responded: YOU ARE ABSOLUTELY RIGHT, SOMETHING SPECIAL INDEED.

That something special was what made my heart skip a beat at the thought of hearing his voice. It seemed like I always reverted back to that girl walking through the hallways of Forrest City High School, hoping that I'd see him before moving on to the next class. Sometimes I did, and sometimes I didn't. But the day was so much better when I did.

♦

The phone was vibrating. I couldn't help but think, *what's going on with my stomach? Butterflies, really Em? It's just Devin.*

Relax. I took a deep breath, and cleared my throat before answering, so I could sound calm and collected.

I answered, "Hello."

"Don't act like you didn't want to talk to me," he joked. "How are you, girl?"

That was the start of a four-hour conversation. We talked about my breakup, and he talked about his relationships and a recent breakup he had experienced. We caught up on work issues and really had a chance to talk about "the celibate life." You see, Devin was the only guy I knew well who had been successful at being celibate for long periods of time. I went to him for advice most of the time, along with some encouragement and prayer.

He asked if I thought it was really over with Brandon, and I told him, "Absolutely."

We finally ended the call in order to get some sleep, and as I fell asleep all I could think of was God leaving us with something special. I said a quick prayer. "Thank you, Lord, for such a good friend," and it was lights out for me.

The next morning, I woke up gasping for air. I sat straight up in my bed and couldn't breathe. As soon as I inhaled and exhaled again, I heard a still small voice say, *"You are going to have to tell him."*

I knew whose voice it was—it was God's. I knew exactly what He was telling me to do. I heard the voice again. *"You are going to have to tell him."* Tears ran down my face at the thought of being obedient to God's voice, and the consequences of actually doing what He said.

♦

See, I had been keeping a secret from Devin all of these years. Back when I'd lived in Forrest City, during the time he was distancing himself from me due to my drinking and rambunctious behavior, I felt desperate. I didn't know how to not lose him, as I felt him slipping farther and farther away from me.

One afternoon, I was talking to a neighbor of mine, a girl in her early twenties, and she was telling me about a time where she had a pregnancy scare, and even though they decided to abort the baby, it brought her and her boyfriend back together stronger than ever, that they had plans to get married and start a family in a few years.

As soon as the girl stopped talking, a lightbulb went off. *Maybe that's how I will get Devin back. I will just lie and tell him I am pregnant, we reunite, I fake an abortion, we stay together and live happily ever after.*

So, I lied to him. Which did nothing but stress the boy out even more. We were seniors at the time, and all he could think about was college and his future and how he didn't feel it was the right time to have a baby. So that was the perfect time for me to say I would have an abortion (to end my fake pregnancy). I scheduled my fake appointment in Memphis, and he asked to take me, but of course, I refused. Once I came back from my fake trip and told him that it was all over, the last thing on his mind was getting back together. It seemed to me like he was relieved, and shortly after, we were finally over… for good.

Even during the time we'd reunited in college, I never told him the truth. I never mentioned it again and it was never talked about. Ever. Completely repressed in my memory.

Reliving that very experience that morning, at least fifteen years later, woken up out of my sleep was very scary. So many memories and conversations had all made sense now. The guilt

Devin had when I really did get pregnant at seventeen by some totally random guy in LA was because of the baby he thought he'd persuaded me to abort. At just twenty, his promise to help me take care of Emani and to help me get my PhD was probably due to that lie that he never got over. I had to tell him the truth. How could I call myself a friend to this man without telling him?

I get it God. I will do it.

So of course, I didn't call him, but I texted him and asked if he had time to read an email I was about to send.

He texted back: WELL, WHY DON'T YOU JUST CALL ME. I'M UP

I responded: SORRY, I'LL SEND AN EMAIL

I typed the email, told him all about the lie, confirmed that the first time I was ever pregnant was with Emani, and that I was sorry. I also told him I could understand if he never forgave me.

He responded about thirty minutes later. Although expected, I could tell he was outraged just by the tone of his email. He confirmed the guilt he'd been saddled with all this time. He even further explained that he had carried that baby with him all of these years, and felt that failed relationships were due to the sin we'd committed years ago. At the end of the email, he said he forgave me, and that he wished me and the girls the best in the future, basically saying, "Have a nice life."

After reading the email, Emani and I had to make a Target run (yes, another dramatic Target run, go figure). During the drive, and as we pulled up to the parking lot, the tears just would not stop running down my face.

"Mommy, what's wrong? Why are you crying?"

I basically gave her the whole rundown. At this point in our lives, I felt that it was appropriate (since she was now 15 or so), to tell her pretty much everything about relationships, about life. As I grew in Christ, I had been taking her along with me.

I told her about the God moment I'd had earlier that morning, and that I'd acted on it and immediately lost a friend. Then she started boo-hoo crying. Now both of us were walking around Target looking crazy.

She said, "Mom, he seemed like the perfect guy for you, and he was willing to take care of me when I was a baby. Wow! I wish I remembered him."

To cheer us up, I told her how he used to fly out to LA during college and put together all of her toys I had stuck in the closet. He would assemble a toy car, put her in it, and zoom her around the living room. Then he'd go off to see whatever else I had around the house for her that was not assembled. It was like he was a kid in a toy chest, just with an added baby to play with. We were both so young, but he was so good to her even back then.

♦

About a month or so after receiving the email, I hadn't heard from Devin. I was missing him more than ever. I wasn't sure why this was a big deal only after a month because sometimes we went a whole year or two without talking to each other. Perhaps it was because I was afraid he would never speak to me again. Perhaps I was mourning the loss of a true friend.

I hadn't dated during that time. I think I just needed some time to get in the Word. I was exhausted. Then it dawned on me. *What if I hadn't lost him?* I decided to text him, and if he didn't respond, then I would know that's the end.

So I sent a text: DEV, HOPE ALL IS WELL. JUST WANTED YOU TO KNOW THAT I MISS TALKING TO YOU.

I ran to the restroom to avoid staring at the phone. I tried to wash some dishes, started sweeping the floor, and was just about to re-arrange my kitchen pantry when I heard a ding. I dropped everything and ran to the phone. It was him.

His response was a pleasant surprise: WELL THEN TALK TO ME BABY GIRL

I called him immediately.

"Hell—"

I cut in right away, "Devin, I am so sorry. I know you said you had forgiven me, but I need you to hear me say it. I am sorry I lied to you. Please, forgive me, friend."

We talked for a few hours that day, every day that week, and that soon became the new normal. Our friendship was still intact; actually, we were closer than ever. Nobody but God could pull off something like that.

One afternoon during our daily conversations, he said, "I think it's time for me to come visit you."

"Are you for real this time? You always say that and then don't come."

"No, for real. I'm serious. I think it's time to come visit."

I thought it was a brilliant idea.

We played around with some dates. It was March 2012, and I threw a date out there for May. I needed to make sure we were doing the right thing. It was evident that the "something special" was a little more than just a friendship. All types of feelings were resurfacing. All I could think was, *I will believe Devin when I see him.*

I recall working out one day at the park, doing a brisk walk, and talking to Dev on the phone. We were talking about what went wrong in our past relationships, and what we would do differently in the next.

He said to me, "Emily, it sounds like you have not been with a man after God's own heart. Please, let me show you what that looks like."

I stopped in my tracks. Only Devin could make a statement like that, so concrete, so confident, so certain. It was definitely a turn-on. The wrong reaction to a statement like that, for sure.

I told him, "Listen, I have a few concerns, *if* we decide to try it again. I need to know that you're going to be faithful if we hit it off, and we need to do the long-distance thing again." (Remembering our challenges back in college).

He said, "Em, if we get back together, I'm not going to cheat on you."

I added, "I want it to be clear—I do not want to have sex with you when you get here. I say that because I'm not confident in myself. I've had too many slipups in my past relationships. I'm not as strong as you are.

Devin sighed. "Em, I am not having sex with you unless you are my wife."

DAMN! This brotha is good. Definitely has a way of shutting me right on up. I was certain of one thing, after being friends with him for many years: If he says he's going to do something, he does it. "Okay, that's all I had."

"Any more questions?"

"Nope, none."

Another time we were having one of our late-night conversations, and he was telling me about his ex-girlfriend, how she just kept breaking up with him over and over again, and that he learned to have a certain level of patience during that relationship.

I thought to myself, "That's just dumb." Well, I thought I said it to myself.

"What's dumb?"

I told him, "I don't understand how anyone would break up with you, let alone repeatedly. She just wasn't the one for you."

"Oh, is that so?"

"Obviously."

"How can you be so certain?"

"Because I am the only one you need in your life. Me. And if it's God's will, I'll be here forever."

He responded, "Well, okay then."

I asked him, "Do you have any more questions?"

"Nope. None."

♦ You may need to be the one to initiate the conversation of celibacy. Don't be afraid to speak up on this.

♦ The one will value your decision, your journey, and most importantly your walk with Christ.

♦ Being friends first, before a relationship, is golden to say the least. Take the time to establish that friendship. You won't regret it.

♦ Whenever you are obedient to God, regardless what it feels like initially, in the long run, it's for your good. That's all for now. Carry on

EVERYTHING

It was finally the day that Devin arrived in LA. Everything was planned perfectly—every outfit, all reservations, the timeline of our outings. I prayed and prayed and prayed that everything would go smoothly. I arrived at the airport from work in my nice black-and-white dress, green cardigan, and pearls. I was going "Michelle Obama" on him this go-around.

I looked around the terminal and couldn't find him. I went back outside and walked toward the location he'd given me. Then I saw a very familiar walk, and then next came the signature ears (think Will Smith) that you couldn't miss for the world. Then there he was, "Jesus's brother", as one of my exes used to call him.

At first glance, he looked older, more mature, his face slimmer. There was something different that I couldn't really put my finger on. I was loving the new beard; in the past, he had always rocked a goatee. I had never considered Devin a pretty boy, but *damn* he was quite handsome. What made him so extraordinary to me was not simply his outward appearance, but what radiated from the inside out, his personality, being a gentleman, his sense of humor, the feeling I got from him when in his presence. Just the overall God in him made me melt. The man still had it, after all of this time. I was super nervous and very anxious.

He greeted me with a hug and took a step back. "Let me check you out."

Of course, I did a quick twirl for him, and he responded with compliments, from that point at the airport, all the way to the car, and the whole time during traffic. Just after fifteen minutes of being around him, I felt like a superstar.

I took him to Roscoe's Chicken and Waffles, keeping up with tradition we had when he used to come to LA years earlier. Always the first stop was Roscoe's. He laughed at how I remembered that. We ate and enjoyed getting reacquainted. It seemed unbelievable that five years had passed since I last sat across from him.

It was time to get him checked into his room. Things were still a bit awkward as I was still so nervous. My nerves just wouldn't calm down for some reason.

As he walked in his room and put his luggage down, I immediately turned away. "Okay, well, you are all set. I will see you later tonight for dinner," and I made a beeline to the door.

He caught my arm as I tried to dash away, pulled me close to his chest, in his arms with one hand, and gently grazed the other hand from the nape of my neck and ran his fingers through my hair. Completely engulfed in this man's arms, he landed the most soft, sweet, gentle kiss on my lips.

Instantly, my body stopped trembling, and my shoulders and fingers were no longer tense. My arms and hands, previously straight down like a mannequin's, were now wrapped around his back. My heartbeat was regular, and my breathing returned back to normal. I swear I still stood there with my eyes closed and my lips puckered long after the kiss was over.

Devin completely calmed my internal storm with just one kiss. *How did he just do that? Amazing.* I thought, *this is going to be a long weekend.*

On the way home from dropping him off at the hotel, and after that passionate kiss that swept me off of my feet right there in his hotel, I got in my car and began to pray immediately, asking God for strength to resist any lust. I basically asked God to "take away my loins."

Just from talking to Devin over the phone for the last few months, I knew for sure he wasn't the same man I'd dated in high school and college. But the attraction was still there. I knew we would need strict boundaries to even get through the weekend. So, here's the plan that I mentally put together:

(1) there'd be no long visits up in the hotel or spending the night

(2) no visits to my house

(3) we'd stay out as much as possible, and

(4) I would stick to my two-drink maximum.

With God's help, if I was able to pull this off, I would know that Devin was a Godsend.

We had the best weekend ever. We dined, we shopped, we went to an upscale, dine-in movie theatre in Pasadena that he loved, and we worked out on the beach. My sister Aretha and I even took him to a popular bowling alley that also had a nice lounge with '90s music. We had cocktails, the three of us danced, left and dropped him right off to the hotel.

"Soooo, what do you think, Re?"

"You two definitely still have something, Em. I almost want to say he's the one. If it turns out to be, make sure you credit me for being the first to say!"

"Alright, sis. I'll let you think you have ESP for tonight. Let's see how the rest of the weekend goes"

A call came in late that Saturday night from him. He said, "Man, it must have been something I ate at the bowling alley. My stomach is upset."

"Do you want me to bring you some medicine?"

"Yes, that'll be great."

You can't imagine how fast I threw together a care package to take to that man. I took a quick shower, shaved, and oiled up before throwing on some sweats to go over there, like I would for a late-night booty call (I guess just out of old habit). When I got there, I made him a quick medicine concoction, which he drank, and we chilled for about ten minutes.

As soon as I said I was heading out, he asked, "Are you tired? Are you up for a movie?"

I quickly changed my mind. "Sure."

Five minutes hadn't passed before our tongues were down each other's throat and we were rolling back and forth on the bed.

I recall looking in his eyes and saying, "I love you." *Damn it! Did I just say that? I wasn't supposed to say it first. Definitely not this weekend.* I just couldn't hold it in; it came out before I could even stop the thought from turning it into words.

He looked surprised at first, and then responded, "I love

you, I do. I love you so much. I never stopped. I always have, I always will."

Thirty minutes went by of even more serious heavy petting. We paused for a second, didn't say a word to each other, and went right back at it. How far did we go? you might be wondering. Well, we ended up performing oral sex on one another, and I'm not sure how, considering we still had all our clothes on.

I left the hotel that night thinking, *Wow! That was fantastic!* At that time, I still felt like we didn't have sex, and I didn't spend the night. You know, the typical "we fooled around but nothing happened" mentality. To me, boundaries were still in place.

♦

We went to church that Sunday.

The pastor said, "Turn to your neighbor and say, 'I've learned something today.'"

We looked at each other, smiled, and gave each other a hug. As I glanced up, with him being much taller, I saw a red mark on his neck. I just shook my head. *Emily, no, you didn't give this man a hickey. Now he's sitting up in church with this thing on his neck.* I just laughed, still not having any remorse from the night before.

We ended our Sunday with a champagne brunch, and a walk around the Marina, watching the yachts float by and listening to the live music in the background. Sunday night was simple, a quick drop-off to his hotel, and I headed home. Besides, I had to pick up the girls from my sister and get them ready for school the next day.

That Monday, as triumphant as I felt, I sat across from him during breakfast with an attitude.

"What's wrong, babe?"

"Oh, nothing."

He just started laughing. "You still act exactly the same as when I used to leave back in the day."

"Oh, really? How is that?"

"Stank! You don't cry, you don't pout, you get an attitude." He busted up laughing in my face.

I couldn't even keep my serious face from laughing. It's funny how he used the word "stank," which I'd heard used so many times before in previous relationships as a flaw of mine. To this man, it was hilarious.

He left that day. We'd kept our boundaries and still had an amazing time. This man had kept his word.

Honestly, had it been up to me entirely, we would have had sex, especially that night with our loins in full effect. I was so consumed that weekend with the idea of Dev and Em possibly being together, being reunited, after all these years. My best friend, my homeboy, the guy that knew everything about me, even my darkest secrets. The guy who had forgiven me for lying to him, putting him on a guilt trip about "our abortion."

Once I dropped him off at the airport and gave him a hug and kiss goodbye, any and all concerns about us being together and him cheating on me were gone. I left him feeling so confident and with a sense of calm and serenity. Hands down, we did it for each other. That weekend was the best. Time with him was just…everything. Literally, everything!

"God's will and His will only" was our catch phrase in college, and twelve years later, the phrase was still relevant. If nothing else, I had a fantastic weekend, with a fantastic man of God.

Lessons Learned

♦ No one said celibacy would be a walk in the park. It is quite the opposite actually.

♦ Yes, God is gracious and merciful but it's not good to test God, saying "how far can we go". This is something I did unconsciously. Try to be all in. Its hard but it's not impossible.

♦ Meeting a great guy (in my case reconnecting with a great one) should be refreshing, and enjoyable. Be anxious for nothing the good book says.

♦ Keep the attitude "God's will and His will only", this will prevent you from over thinking things.

♦ It must be true what Granny used to say…I let him go, and 12 years later, he came back, a totally new man. No coercion, no ultimatums, no pursuing him. He came back to me, on his own. Go figure.

CLOSER

It didn't take long after Devin returned home for us to have "the conversation." We discussed how the weekend went, how we had a good time, and I believe by the second conversation, he asked, "Would you officially be my girlfriend, again?"

"Of course, I will," I replied, laughing. *Long-distance relationship again? Will this work out, with me being in Cali and him being two thousand miles away in Arkansas? What about our living arrangements in the future? Would he be willing to move?*

Mind you, we had been through this before, but the difference was, now we weren't starving college students. But being the budget-savvy guy Devin was, we had to determine how we would fund these visits, considering his first visit ran him about a thousand dollars. Yeah, that wasn't going down every visit, not with this guy. With our new commitment to each other, and dedication to make our long distance relationship work, we decided to establish what we called a "Destiny Fund". Both of us would make deposits bi-weekly to a savings account, and we would use that for our upcoming trips so it wouldn't be taxing on just one person. But because of my financial circumstances at the time—tight budget, and paying off debt—I didn't have very much to contribute to the Destiny Fund anyway. However, Devin was debt-free, and could make substantially more contributions toward the fund than I could. Although I wish I could do more, just making my small contributions showed him how thankful and appreciative I was and that I was just as dedicated on making this work as he was. I made sure to verbally express this as well.

By this time, my eldest daughter Emani was weeks away from finishing the ninth grade at a performing arts high school. There was no way I was going to move her to Arkansas at this age, because that was the very age I'd moved to Arkansas from LA, and my whole world had changed with that move—I had lost my virginity and ended up in an abusive relationship with Mason. So, yes, baggage from my past carried over to my very strict stance on not moving to Arkansas while Emani was in high school, who was doing so well studying dance and not interested in boys at the time.

Devin understood, but he certainly didn't say, "Sure, I'll move to California. No problem."

See, Devin loved the South, so nothing about California appealed to him. He liked fishing, and running around in army fatigues in the woods, with a gun and hunting dogs. So putting my foot down about not moving from California was big. My plan was to stay in California until Emani graduated, and then I would've been open to move from there, just not back to Arkansas. So that's something he had to think about.

And I had to think about a lot as well. Although Devin's laid-back demeanor was perfect when trying to stay holy during courtship, I wasn't sure I could handle his disposition forever in a marriage. I often asked myself, *Is he too godly?* See, I liked to hang out, and I liked to party, but he rarely ever had a drink, didn't like to party, and preferred being home than out and about. Matter of fact, he thought the lounge at the bowling alley I took him to was an actual club.

I wondered, *Would I get bored with this dude?* I mean, we had a blast that weekend, but that was for a weekend after which we weren't going to see each other again for a while.

Then I didn't know if the kids would like him or if he would like them. I thought having good chemistry with the girls was very important. He had visited twice already and hadn't yet met the kids, and I could tell he was comfortable in that place. A family reunion in Arkansas was coming up about ninety minutes away from where he lived, so I thought that would be the perfect opportunity for him to meet the girls, and the rest of my immediate family.

Well, he made the trip, and the girls finally got a chance to meet "my good friend from high school" I had been talking about for the past few months. Emani especially was excited to meet the "perfect guy" we had cried over that day in Target. Kennedy, my seven-year-old, didn't have a clue what was going on. However, my cousin, who did know the real deal, offered to take a picture of the four of us. When gathering for the photo, my youngest daughter ran up to him, wrapped her arms around him and my oldest and started smiling for the photo, as if she had known him for years. It was a little awkward for all of us, but he played it off well, I must say. He met the rest of the family and got reacquainted with both my mom and dad who hadn't seen him in quite a while.

From that point on, future trips to California also consisted of date nights with the girls. Devin had a thing that every time he took me out on a date, the girls would also have to have a date. Which was totally fine with me. They seemed to get along with him very well, Emani a little more than Kennedy. Emani got along with everyone, but Kennedy wasn't quite as social. She was also very close to her own father, so she must have had some reservations about getting too close to him. I watched her physically pull back in her emotions, in a sense, checking herself, out of respect for her dad, and Devin eventually picked up on that too.

In a short period of time, the girls both had pictures posted in their rooms from photo booths with all four of us in them, and some with just them three. One even had "Daddy's Little Girl" on the header, which the girls had picked out themselves. For that to be posted in Kennedy's room in particular, was just priceless.

Devin was frugal, and I liked to spend. I wasn't sure this would work, especially for a girl who was used to being wined and dined. One day he and I were in an upscale mall in Los Angeles with high-end boutiques and stores. We went into the Louis Vuitton store, and I immediately started trying on bags.

Devin was cheering me on. "Oooh, babe, that one looks good on you. What about the bigger one?"

He had the whole store in there swarming around us at this point, like he was Floyd Mayweather or somebody. He finally found a bag that he really liked, the one all the way at the top of the shelf, and once I put it on he asked the clerk, "How much is it?"

"This one is fifty-eight hundred, sir."

He paused for a second.

I was holding my breath at the time, and had the biggest grin on my face. *I'm about to get treated to this beautiful bag.*

"Oh, okay. Thank you, ma'am. Em, are you ready?"

Just like that, I was taking that bag off my shoulder and handing it back to the clerk, and he was kindly escorting me right on up out of that LV store. I was so embarrassed.

"Almost six thousand dollars for a bag? That's just crazy. Who would pay so much for a purse? That's just absurd."

I thought, *Oh, well ... there goes my fantasy of having a baller husband to take me shopping and spending thousands of dollars on me.* Yes, materialistic I know, but hey, that was my fantasy, okay.

I had to come to terms with the fact that the man I was dating didn't spend frivolously. However, it wasn't a deal-breaker.

The more I thought about he and I possibly getting married, the more I worried about my financial situation. My credit was in the low 500's, and I had 100K+ in debt that I was paying about $100 extra toward a month, while making small contributions to our fund. Meanwhile, Devin had an almost 800 credit score, no debt, money saved, and was still able to contribute substantially toward our Destiny fund. I wanted to have my financial situation out of the way and under control before getting married, and I was nowhere close.

Pretty soon, anxiety started creeping in. I began ranting and raving to him, saying, "Go ahead, free yourself (in my Fantasia voice), find yourself a nice, successful woman with no kids, no debt, with a fat savings account. I have too much baggage."

Devin asked, "What the heck started all of this? Is it something I said?" Then he added, "If things progress, and we get married, your debt would be *our* debt. Good thing I have good credit to hold us down."

Also, I wasn't sure if we could remain celibate until marriage, especially not knowing when that would be. We'd been dating for about six or seven months with no major drama. Our boundaries were set: no spending the night at the hotel room, staying out as much as possible during his visits. We saw each other about every six weeks. Though it worked for us, I believe both of us wanted more of each other.

I started to become curious about his life in Little Rock, Arkansas, so we scheduled my first visit to see him. He was a little tardy, showing up at the airport looking like Will Smith in *Hancock* with his long trench coat, white T-shirt, and jeans, but from behind his back came a gift bag with a nice "Welcome to Little Rock" gift.

On the drive to his apartment, my anxiety started kicking in. This trip was going to be quite different—I would be staying at his apartment, and there wouldn't be any kids around—so definitely our commitment to being celibate would be tested.

We tried to keep the weekend jam-packed with activities. We would visit my mother's old house out in the country, about forty-five minutes away, to pick up a few sentimental items. Then we would end the night visiting his mom as well, since it was in the same neck of the woods. Saturday would be for us, possibly visit some of his friends, and then it would be off to church bright and early Sunday morning, lunch, and off to the airport.

We went to his apartment for me to "wash off" the airport and to change clothes. Well, I soon found out that "celibacy + shower + alone-time in an apartment = drama." Our hormones were raging—no, on fire.

"Can you bring me a towel for the shower?" turned into "Let me turn the shower on for you," which turned into "Let me help you take your clothes off," which turned into a butt-naked, hot and steamy make out session.

"Sessions" were what we called oral sex at this point. They didn't happen every time he visited, but probably every other time. Devin managed to make it out that bathroom without violating our pact. He excused himself, and I locked the door behind him and turned the shower from hot to cold.

We met my cousin to let us in to my grandmother's old abandoned house. It had been ten years since anyone had been there. As soon as we drove down that long dirt road, memories of my teenage years came flooding back—Yelling and screaming matches with my stepfather; being taken away by police car, which eventually led me to a foster home for eighteen months; and finding my mother face down in the trailer after overdosing on medication during her second suicide attempt.

I immediately filed those memories away. "Let's get in and out of here." I told Devin and my cousin that my mom was looking for photo albums and old family photos that had been left abandoned in the house.

The two guys looked at each other and said "alright, let's do this" and went in that rundown house, full of animal feces and trash, where people had looted the house over the years, while I sat in the car, to save myself from mosquitoes. About 30 minutes later, Devin came and knocked on the window and asked me to come in.

I went to the broken door of the house, and there they were, four or five photo albums, other objects from my old room, and even some of my school papers. I thought, *Wow, he did it. Well, they did it.*

That was something that me and my sisters hadn't been able to pull off all this time. Even guys in my immediate family weren't willing to go into an abandoned house, pull up their sleeves, and look for things on behalf of my mother. Not only did Devin do so much for me, but also for my kids, and now for my mother. I had never met a man so selfless. At that very moment, I really felt deep down inside that he was the one.

That night we spent hours sitting on his kitchen floor going through old pictures, laughing at old outfits and pictures of me holding up dead possums or planting rows of peas.

He busted out laughing. "You really are a country girl! Wait until your Cali friends see these."

The rest of the trip went fairly well too. The trip to visit his mom went better than expected. Those two were very, very close, him being the only child and all. So I was a bit concerned about that.

When we were about to leave, his mom gave me a big hug and said to me, "I am so glad you two are back together."

Devin threw in a surprise the following day, which was Saturday. We actually went ring-shopping. I had never looked at engagement rings before and was elated at the idea of going to put diamonds on my finger. Every ring I picked up was worth 25K or more. I didn't realize I had such expensive taste. Remember, Devin was very frugal. I doubted very seriously I was getting a ring worth that much. But I didn't care; I could hear wedding bells in the back of my head. The fact that he was getting an idea of what I wanted was a plus. I couldn't believe this was happening.

Visits with friends went well too. I couldn't bowl worth a damn, but we had a great time.

After church Sunday morning, Devin carried me around, introducing me to this person and that person. I was greeted with "I heard so much about you" by so many people, it was unbelievable.

♦

As we sat there at lunch before my flight took off, I couldn't help but to confirm that my trip was a success. I felt welcomed into his world, and left Little Rock with no reservations about our long-distance relationship. I trusted him, and that was a very good feeling indeed.

♦ As you get closer, be careful to not self-sabotage your relationship with your own negativity, self-doubt and/or insecurities. These often come up when things appear to be "too good to be true."

♦ Always remember that you are the QUEEN and you deserve a KING. Just because you have been meeting frogs all of your life, or that your crown is a little dusty, doesn't mean that once royalty comes along, you are not deserving.

♦ Yes, you will have some reservations when you meet the one. I listed several that I had during this courtship, however, when its true love, you will question it, but just shortly. Soon, God will give you the confirmation that everything is just the way He has set it up, for our own good.

♦ Good relationships flow with a natural progression, with some tests and trials along the way. The difference is, the trial will be followed by a positive outcome, or will bring the two of you closer than you were before.

♦ Think of courtship as a test that you take. You may not get ALL of the answers correct...you can miss a few, and still get an A. #winning

Chapter 18

SAY YES

After I returned to LA from that trip to Arkansas, we couldn't go long without acknowledging how crazy that shower incident was. We started to question how serious we were about being celibate, how important it was for our relationship, and could we keep it up. If we did, we were going to have to take things to another level. Devin had a good idea for us to find a devotional book for couples who wanted to abstain from sex.

He called me up and said, "Found a book, babe. I ran across it at Barnes and Noble—*Sex, Dating, and Relationships* by this author named Gerald Hiestand. I think it's interesting, but I'm not sure you'll like it."

"Why not?"

"Man, it's heavy. Radical. I've read over half of it just sitting here."

"What! What's it about? Go ahead and read me a passage."

"All right. 'God calls us to reserve our sexuality for the marriage relationship, because it is only in marriage that the image of

Christ's relationship to the church can be lived out.'"

"Oookkaaayyy, we're doing that. What's the big deal?"

"That's not the crazy part."

"Uh-oh." I knew deep down he was going to bring up our "sessions." I just knew it.

Devin continued to read: "'Clearly, sexual relations extend beyond sexual intercourse. Oral sex, fondling, and mutual masturbation, for example, are all sexual activities.'"

Long pause on my end.

"Babe, you still there?"

"Yeah, I'm here. Go on."

"'Clearly, some forms of kissing are nonsexual. We kiss our children and our mothers. But there are some forms of kissing that we reserve exclusively for our wives. And the reason we do so is precisely that those forms of kissing are sexual.'"

Devin cleared his throat and continued '"God calls us to absolute purity. Let's not put even a toe in the water of sexual immorality. Single people are called to celibacy. Not partial celibacy, but complete celibacy.'"

"Oh, heck nah! Who the heck wrote this? That's crazy to me! We can't even kiss? That book is dumb."

♦

I couldn't sleep at all that night. I woke up and ordered it from Amazon, and asked for overnight shipment. I received it and spent the weekend reading it.

As soon as I read the last line, an immediate conviction came over me—our "sessions" were sexual sin. Although we hadn't had sexual intercourse as I understood it, we were engaging in sexual sin. We had been pulling a "Bill Clinton" this whole time. The sessions had to go.

I dropped down to the floor of my room, on my knees, face down, tears running down my cheeks and started to pray. *"Lord, please forgive me for I have sinned. I am trying, and You have showed me yet another thing to take away in order to obey You. Lord, just take away my loins, Lord God. Take them away. I want this to work. I want to obey you. I love sessions, but I love You more, though. Sorry I said that, but You know my heart.*

"If Devin is for me, we can stop. I can do all things, Lord God, with you! Thank you, Father, for leading Devin to this book. Thank you for not letting us carry on like this. We will do better. Whatever you want me to do to make this work, my answer is YES. I will SAY YES. Amen."

♦

After making another pact with each other to stop the sessions, things began to take off at God's speed. Devin started to apply for jobs here in Los Angeles, and within a few months, he received a very lucrative job offer.

It was now late July 2013, and Devin was on the road to California, with the U-Haul trailer right behind. I had found him an apartment close to his job in Irvine, in the next county over, about forty miles away. Sure, I could have tried to find something closer, but the whole time I kept thinking, *No more sessions, no more sessions.* So, yeah, Irvine was fine.

Our first Sunday together after he moved, it was the altar call at church.

Devin politely said, "Let's go."

I felt like I was getting dragged down to the front, trying to keep up with his long strides in my three-inch heels.

When other altar workers tried to approach us for prayer, Devin said, "No, we want to talk to Bishop."

A lady sitting in the front row saw us trying to shoo the other saints away. She got out of her seat, grabbed our hands, and pulled us to the side of the stage. She signaled Bishop Ulmer to the side and said to him, "This couple wants prayer."

Devin didn't waste any time. "Bishop, I just moved to LA for this woman. I don't want to have sex with her before making her my wife. Please pray for us."

And, sure enough, my Bishop, who had led me spiritually for the past ten years, laid hands on us and prayed.

I looked at Devin a little differently that day. I left that altar with my boyfriend, feeling more confident than just moments before. *We can do this,* I thought to myself. Or maybe it was God telling me, *"You can do this."*

♦

About two weeks after Devin had moved, he said, "I want to treat you and the girls to a day of shopping and fun with my first paycheck."

Girls being girls, you know we were down for that. He met us out here in LA, and we were off. We shopped our hearts out, ate, and shopped some more. We had a blast.

When we got home, I was exhausted. As I sat relaxing in the living room, I heard Devin calling the girls into the living room with me. *Damn!* I thought. *There goes my little peace and quiet.*

"Girls, Em, the four of us need to debrief about the day."

"What's *debrief*?" Kennedy asked.

Devin responded, "Recap, reflection—what you liked most about the day, what you didn't like."

So, the girls went on to say how much they enjoyed the day.

He looked at me. "Well, what about you, Mom?"

"Yeah, it was great! Thank you so much, babe, for treating us. I'm just a little tired, but yeah, I had a blast."

"Well, it wasn't that great for me," he said.

We all turned and looked at him in puzzlement.

"What do you mean, babe? What? You spent too much money?"

"No, babe, it's just that although it was family appreciation day, so to speak, I didn't feel like I was officially a part of the family. But I think I can fix that. Can you stand for a minute?"

"Okay."

Then he dropped down on one knee and took this small black box out of his pocket. I immediately covered my mouth to muffle my scream.

The girls began to scream on my behalf.

Then he said, "Will you marry me, Emily?"

At that moment, I let out the scream I was trying so desperately to hold in. The girls and I then formed a group hug and started jumping up and down, chanting, "We are getting married, we are getting married!"

Devin cleared his throat. "Hello? Is that a yes?"

I laughed. The man was still down on one knee. "Yes, baby, yes!"

Devin jumped up and gave me the biggest hug, swirling me in the air.

Lessons Learned

♦ Even in a relationship that is going "good", if God tells you to do something different, do it. If he tells you no, respect his answer. This level of obedience is imperative to the next level that he wants to take you to, although you might be in your own way.

♦ Saying YES to God will get your closer to saying YES to your soulmate, faster than any and all dating tips that I have provided throughout this book.

♦ When you do say yes, just sit back and witness how fast God moves. God's timing is perfect.

Recessional

UNTIL THE END OF TIME

On July 27, 2014, two years after Devin's first visit to LA, one year after he proposed, I married the man of my dreams, with 150 of our closest friends and family present, and my two daughters front and center. My daughters bore witness to a man brought into their mother's life, into their lives, sent and ordained by God.

Oh, and I can't go without mentioning…our wedding night was simply….amazing! The two years, two months and twenty-two days that we held out, was definitely all worth it. It was the first time ever, in 20 years, that I felt absolutely no guilt, shame or uncertainty afterwards. Instead, I felt revived, rejoiceful, triumphant, secure, and completely sprung out on a man who was mine. Not just for one night, for the moment, in the meantime; no, this time it would be forever. I'll leave it at this, almost three years and counting, I have not been disappointed yet. The love that I have for this man gets stronger and stronger with every encounter. *I get it God,* I often think to myself, *I totally get why You have designed sex for marriage.* It's the glue that keeps us together, keeps us striving, keeps us growing. Now, those are all the details you get ladies. This is my forever love we are talking about. I don't want to have to hurt anybody (smile).

♦

The stories within this book have been shared with my eldest daughter, and will be with the rest of my children the moment they are of age to understand. The concept of devoting their lives to God and making their bodies a living sacrifice is being reiterated in our homes daily. My eldest daughter, now 19, is keeping up her end of our pact that we made when she was 14 and I was single at 32 to save ourselves and remain celibate until marriage. I had tried everything. But listening to God's voice, and my decision to obey that command was the best thing I could have ever done.

♦

So now, my sister, as promised in the beginning of this book, my goal was to get you closer to the altar. However, that altar is not the one you walk down with your groom. It's the "spiritual altar", the one where you lay all of your burdens and sins at God's feet. It's the "mental aisle" you'll walk down to get closer to God.

For the single person, sexual purity is like being on a fast, abstaining from something our flesh is yearning for in order to save it for God's purpose. Will you make that same commitment? Will you vow to remove sex from your life completely until after your wedding day?

There are plenty of benefits to this, as I have mentioned throughout the book. Dating relationships were better; in fact, my entire life got better, the more and more my relationship with God became the priority. Yet the greatest benefit was to be able to hear God's voice clearly during our courtship, and to repeatedly hear Him say, *"That's the one."*

When you surrender yourself to God, all blessings flow. It

may not look like it right away, but then healing from years and years of toxic relationships begins to take place. Suddenly, the same unhealthy types of men are no longer approaching you and asking you out, and if they do, you have a new sense of discernment to not even waste your time. Your own personal desires and goals begin to mimic the desires of God's own heart and not your own.

You want change? God can give that to you. You want more? God can provide more. You want love? God is love. It's through Him, and only Him, that I was blessed to marry my best friend. My "happily-ever-after" did not come until then.

Many marriages take place without celibacy, and good long-term marriages at that. I could have been married years ago, working it out, waiting it out with past relationships. But that's not what I wanted. I didn't want what was good, I wanted God's best.

I love that sexual purity is now becoming cool—DeVon Franklin and Meagan Good; Ciara and Russell Wilson; Brelyn and Tim Bowman, Jr. and countless other couples. Then there's me, your girl next door, just another chick from LA with Arkansas roots, here to say that celibacy was the best thing that ever happened to me.

So, again, if God's best is what you want, what are you willing to do to get it? Better yet, what are you willing to NOT do to get the desires of your heart? I can never express enough how merciful God is. He showed me exactly what NOT to DO before saying I DO, and now I have the pleasure of sharing all of these DON'Ts with you. This wasn't by accident. This was divine assignment at its best. If He did this for me, with all of my mess, my sister, He can do it for you. I pray that you make the best decision for you, and that God's plan for you becomes your plan. There's hope for the romantic, my friend, and that hope is in Him.

Notes

CHAPTER	SONG TITLE REFERENCE	ARTIST
Prelude	Hello	Adele
1	If It Isn't Love	New Edition
2	All I Do is Think of You	Troop
3	Beautiful Liar	Rhianna
4	Upgrade You	Beyoncé
5	Blessing in the Storm	Kirk Franklin
6	Flaws and All	Beyoncé
7	How Come You Don't Call Me	Alicia Keys
8	Just Friends	Musiq Soulchild
9	He Will Restore	VaShawn Mitchell
10	How Many Drinks?	Miguel
11	Make Me Over	Tonex
12	Superpower	Beyoncé
13	Bills, Bills, Bills	Destiny's Child
14	On to the Next	Jay-Z
15	Butterflies	Alicia Keys
16	Everything	Mary J. Blige
17	Closer	Floetry
18	Say Yes	Shekinah Glory
Recessional	Until the End of Time	Beyoncé

Chapter 18: Say Yes

Hiestand, G., & Thomas, J. S. (2012). *Sex, Dating, and Relationships: A Fresh Approach*. Crossway.

Free Gift For You

Authors **Devin** and **Emily McKnight**, share a very intimate and transparent guide to dating while celibate. Celibacy, with its growing popularity, still remains quite a mystery and challenge for individuals who have spent years living a sexual lifestyle. This couple shares the tools that any single person, regardless of their past, will need to be successful at being celibate.

Whether you are single, dating, in a relationship or engaged, Devin and Emily candidly answers every question imaginable around the topic; sharing their personal stories, pain points and most importantly, how they made it through.

This couple is not only relatable, but has a sure passion for helping others succeed. In this e-book, you will gain the answers to the following questions and much more:

What is celibacy?

Where do I start?

How do I date while celibate?

How far is too far?

When to have "the talk"?

What boundaries to put into place to be successful?

What to do if I fail?

Visit www.takeitfromem.com/celibacy to download your free copy.

SIA information can be obtained
www.ICGtesting.com
nted in the USA
DW01n1854220617
46FS

9 780997 593105

CI
at
Pri
FS
35

Free Gift For You

Authors **Devin** and **Emily McKnight**, share a very intimate and transparent guide to dating while celibate. Celibacy, with its growing popularity, still remains quite a mystery and challenge for individuals who have spent years living a sexual lifestyle. This couple shares the tools that any single person, regardless of their past, will need to be successful at being celibate.

Whether you are single, dating, in a relationship or engaged, Devin and Emily candidly answers every question imaginable around the topic; sharing their personal stories, pain points and most importantly, how they made it through.

This couple is not only relatable, but has a sure passion for helping others succeed. In this e-book, you will gain the answers to the following questions and much more:

What is celibacy?

Where do I start?

How do I date while celibate?

How far is too far?

When to have "the talk"?

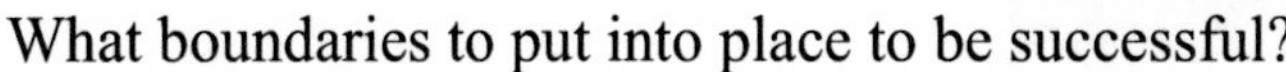

What boundaries to put into place to be successful?

What to do if I fail?

Visit www.takeitfromem.com/celibacy to download your free copy.

CPSIA information can be obtained
at www.ICGtesting.com
Printed in the USA
FSOW01n1854220617
35546FS